Liberal Arts Electives

By Cari Lynn Vaughn

Liberal Arts Elective Introduction

I began classes at The Ohio State University at Mansfield the Fall of 1994. I took a number of English classes during my five years there. I published all the notes from those classes in the book Baccalaureate in Arts. As anyone who has been to college knows, the classes you take for your Major only comprise a fraction of the overall requirements.

No matter what degree is sought, Freshman Composition and Math are always part of the list. History and Science are also required for Liberal Arts Degree, but I have not included them here. For the record, I took *World History* 110 and 111. I also took *Geology* and *Oceanography.* My notes from *Oceanography* inspired my book *The Physics of Emotions.*

One of the first classes I took was Introduction to *Psychology* with Dr. Fisher, but I found the nuts and bolts of the science uninspiring. I was hoping to dive into Freud, Jung and Lacan, but no such luck. I would have been thrilled to learn how to counsel people or learn to create a profile of criminal, but all those were upper level classes not offered at OSU-M. I did not keep my notes from *Introduction to Psychology.*

The Fall of 1995 I took *Anthropology* with Dr. McLeod, which I enjoyed a great deal. I want to take *Archaeology*, but it was not offered. *Anthropology* turned out to be an interesting class, and I was glad I had signed up.

The Winter of 1995, I took *Introduction to Sociology.* Although the text was pretty dry, I loved our classroom discussion. The professor had lead an interesting life and welcomed discussions that didn't always center on the text. I probably would have done better in that class if we had had tests over the discussions instead of the reading!

The Winter of 1996, I took *Elements of Japanese Culture* with Jennifer Dell-Armstrong to fulfill one of my many electives. I had always been drawn to Japan and was excited to learn more about its history and culture. I would have loved to have traveled to Japan, but the class was the closest I was going to get. It proved to be a wonderful experience and I even did well in that class.

In the Spring of 1996, I took *African Art and Archaeology.* Although I didn't know much about African countries or culture, I thought the class would be interesting, and it was. This was a subject I probably wouldn't have researched on my own, but it turned out to be an eye-opening experience.

The Winter of 1997 I took *Introduction to Philosophy.* Those notes are not included here. My notes weren't great for the class, but parts of them ended up being a part of my book *Sophia's Wiki.* Much of what I learned from Philosophy was from books I read on my own. I loved diving into the life and mind of particular Philosophers. The General Survey class I took didn't do much for me. When I was able to apply particular philosophies and philosophers to Literature, it really helped open up the subject for me though. In Graduate School I took a *Critical Canon* class, which did just that and I excelled in that class!

The Summer of 1998 I took *Sociology of the Family* with Dr. Burke. As with his Introductory Class, I found the readings ho-hum, but the classroom discussions were lots of fun.

Finally, the Fall of 1998 I took *History of Germany in the 20th Century* with Dominic. Even though I had trouble memorizing names and dates, I loved History. Going in depth with a particular time and place was even ended up being an even better experience than what I had with the general survey courses.

Especially with what has happened in the USA since 2016, I found that class to be perhaps the most relevant of all. I feel like if more people had been required to take History of Germany in the 20th Century, this whole debacle might have been avoided. The saying, "*Those who do not know their history are doomed to repeat, it,*" is quit accurate.

Many college students feel like these Electives are stupid or have nothing to do with their degree. The idea of a Liberal Arts Degree has always been to create a well-rounded person. It is about widening or changing the Student's perspective of the world. And it did just that. But the Liberal Arts Electives also allowed me to gain inspiration and explore paths I wouldn't have been able to otherwise. The tendency these days is to train for a specific skill, but in doing so, students miss out personal growth and enrichment. People fail to see the practicality of learning about other people and cultures. While learning a trade can earn a student money, getting a Liberal Arts Degree can give them a sense of the world they live in.

Cultural Anthropology
Anthropology 202

Instructor: James Robert McLeod (Died November 1998)
Office Bromfield 289
Class Meeting: 12:30pm to 1:30pm M-Th
Fall 1995

Required Texts:
Contemporary Culture Anthropology by Howard
Yanomamo: The Fierce People by Chagnon, 1983, 3rd Edition

Course Description: Welcome To Cultural Anthropology. This course is designed to aquatint you with the fundamental insights and findings of the science of humankind, anthropology. It is an integrative course covering the experience of humanity in both cross temporal and cross-cultural perspective. We will briefly survey several cultures around the world, analyzing such diverse aspects of culture as kinship, politics, religion, myths, folk tales and various dimensions of social change. This is not a course in how humans should live, but rather a give course in how humans have lived and do live. Our purpose is to give the student an understanding of those processes which have led to the present cultures around the world interact with each other, and how culture affect you.

About The Course: Cultural Anthropology is one of the four major sub-fields in Anthropology as it is it is taught

Week 1: Introduction

Announcement: *There is Anthropology Club meeting on October 10th in Ovalwood 147 at 5pm. Be there if you are interested in joining.*

Cultural Anthropology is the study of the Global Community and Cultures Around the World. There are 180 countries and some 1,000 cultures. Glottochronoogy is the shift in language over time. For example, from Pater to Father and Philistine to Palestine.

Culture is a way of life specific to a certain group of people.

Ethnicity or Ethnocentric-ism is people thinking that their culture is the only culture and the best culture. It is difficult to find an idea that is considered "right" among all cultures. Culture is a lens that you see the world with. It colors what you hear, see, taste, and smell as well your actions and attitudes.

Cultural Relativism is every cultural system should be judged upon its own values and beliefs, not your own. "All cultures are existentially equal." You can't morally judge other cultures. However, there is an argument to be had that we did the right thing in persecuting the Germans for the Holocaust. To be fair the Trials at Nuremberg were held by Germans against Germans though. There is also a book on the Japanese Kamikaze Pilots of WWII called *Thundergods.* The book points out that committing an honorable suicide was part of their culture and they did so voluntarily.

The Socialization Process is a long and complicated one. It is within all about learning how to exist within a society and grow. Toilet training is pretty universal, but how and when it happens is different from culture to culture. Culture can also be considered an environment of predictable rules. Culture is a place of many unwritten rules. Learning these rules makes life less chaotic and is important for "fitting in." When culture begins to breaks down, there is massive social change.

The Hippies made a change in American Culture when they spoke out against the Vietnam War. The chaos they created led to a positive change. It created a revolution.

Culture by E Adamson Hoebel, "*Culture is an integrated system of learned patterns of behavior, which are characteristic of members of a society, and which are not the result of biological inheritance, not genetically predetermined and non-instinctual. It is wholly the result of social invention and transmitted or learned through communication.*"

According to Leslie White, a Social Anthropologist, "*Culture is an extra-somatic body or out of the body continuum. Things and events are dependent upon symbolizing specifically and concreting culture consists of tools, utensils, ornaments, customs, rituals, institutions, clothing, beliefs, language and works of art.*"

Human nature says it is in our genes or our blood. Maxwell Anderson is credited with the idea of the "bad seed." It is a widespread belief that there is something wrong with the person's race or bloodline. Then came the idea that bad or taboo deeds came from a person's environment and not their biology. Environment vs Biology is a topically that is a subject of intense debate among professionals. For the purpose of this class, we will focus on Environment and how it shapes the people within in it.

There have been four important discoveries. Sigmund Freud was the first to talk about the subconscious, dreams, neurosis, psychosis and other things. Einstein's Theory of Relativity helped the general public to understand the way the Physical World. His ideas not only expanded Newton's ideas, but also overturned them. Watson and Crick discovered the Double Helix of DNA. Our relationship to each other and the world changed with this. We are all water in somebody's ocean.

We take for granted our cultural beliefs, customs and clothes. In any case, we need 6 things to survive. The first is biological functioning--aka Health. We also must reproduce to have new members of our group. When the Shakers outlawed intercourse, they were unable to keep the Shakers going. Abortion and Infanticide also go against this need to replace the old and dying of a specific culture. It is also important to socialize young children into society. We do this by passing knowledge down from older generation to younger generations. Teen suicide counteracts this. We produce and distribute goods and services needed for life. MOP is defined as Means of Production. It is all about who get what, where, when and how. The fifth thing vital to cultural survival is maintaining order in the group. Conflict is a fact of life, but a successful culture finds equilibrium. The sixth and final thing for cultural survival is meaning. Everyone must engage in meaningful activities that make sure the group will continue to thrive in the world.

Some topics in our culture that were polled upon or tested in our recent presidential election include smoking policies, public schools, prison policy, welfare policies and God in Politics. The Separation of Church and State has been a source of conflict in culture in recent years.

Week 2: Field World, The Yanomamo and Warfare

The Yanamamo or Yanomami live in Venezuela and Northern Brazil. They live in a part of the Amazon Rain Forest that is dense and mostly unmapped. Each village is about a 3 to 4 day walk apart from the other villages. Some of their land has been deforested due to the slash and burn policies of the government there.

A young Missionary visited there. The airfield was a cleared flat area. They live on a branch of the Amazon called the Yonoko River. Along with the Missionary a linguist, photographer and dentist, they studied the tribe. Banana is their main crop. Malaria and Yellow Fever are common there. They have twice as many children as adults. They dress in loincloths, with feathered armbands and have painted bodies. They have cropped black hair and often sport necklaces.

Groups of Yanomami live in villages usually consisting of their children and extended families. Villages vary in size, but usually contain between 50 and 400 native people. In this largely communal system, the entire village lives under a common roof called the *sabono*. *Shabonos* have a characteristic oval shape, with open grounds in the center measuring an average of 100 yards (91m). The *shabono* shelter constitutes the perimeter of the village

They hunt by slashing and burning. All but the largest trees are cut down. The brush and small trees are burned. Crops are planted where possible. Each family has a plot to call their own. They also grow maize (corn), peach trees, palm trees, tobacco and cotton. Drugs and magical mushrooms also grow there. Children play as both parents work to plant more crops. The kids snack on bananas. Sometimes they smash the banana to a pulp on a leaf to eat it. They also eat raw insects. Sometimes they will boil or roast caterpillars and other insects in leaves to eat.

The natives groom and preen each other. They pick out the lice from each other's hair. Children put burs in their hair as decorations. The women spin cotton and the men trade it. The girls wear skirts and sometimes have leg and wristbands. The men will have 3 or 4 arrows each. The shaft is made from a dried plant. Turkey feathers or some other bird feather will be attached to the end.

The adult men will snuff hallucinogenic each day. It is painful to snort at first. Then the drug feels good. During the trip they chant, fiddle, dance and get ready for warfare. Lots of Indians will die in warfare. Most of them will die of illness and disease though.

The day the feast they clean the village. They prepare a large amount of food--mostly Banana Paste. They store it in the back of a tree trough. Children decorate each other and their pets. When the visitors arrive, they dance first. The men dance in pairs and split away to show others their finery and then the entire group dances.

The groups drink from trough with bowls. Sometimes there is controlled fighting and violence. They are intoxicated and need the release. At dusk the host and guests began chanting. They chant all night long together. This cements their friendship and they a free to trade with each other.

The day of the raid against their enemy they will paint themselves with charcoal. They often drink the cremated remains of their friends. Women will drink the remains of the men killed in battle later on. Anyway, Men yell and then leave. They vow to find their enemy. Women weep for the potential loss of thief mates and family members. The name of their loved ones who die in battle are never spoken again.

There is a race to save the Yanamamo. Missionaries give vaccinations. The Collapse of the village life due to modern interference may kill them quicker than disease though. Still, they need access to antibiotics and the like. Doctors take blood samples and saliva samples to test them. The impressions they take of their teeth also provide information. Patterns of wear on their teeth tell us a lot about their lives. Genes can be linked to their tribe, environment and culture.

Anthropologists also make note of birth rates, death rates, migration, marriage and anything else they can find out. It is difficult to get their history when Yanamamo have about average birth and death rates. The Indians think the Anthropologists are weird for taking stool samples. The samples give us great insight into their diet and overall health. It is determined these natives are in good health.

Week 3 Kinship, Marriage and Society

Kinship is confusing. Americans confuse sex, marriage, family and kinship for love. In the Presidential Debate of 1992 there was a focus on Family Values by Republicans. There is a big difference between the Ideal Family and the Reality of Family. People tend to lump categories all together, but anthropologists try to separate and define these things.

Today to stay married is highly unusual. Divorce has become the norm. Even still, we have this ideal in our heads that we should stay blissfully married until we die. This just isn't realistic. Soap Operas represent our ideals, minus the morals. Soaps often give us conflicting messages about kinship, sex, marriage, family and love.

Most people in America believe in the ideal of marriage, but behave in completely contradictory way. It is not just in American though.

"On the ground" means operating below emotions, in just instinct. Culture provides an ideal to live by and our reality is what we often refer to as "society."

On the book about the Yanomamo they talked about how the Amazon tribe played with his mind. They didn't always tell him the truth. Sometimes they lied. They refused to tell him tell him the names of their own dead or the names of people in the other villages. On the other side of that, the missionaries told the tribe members that their way of doing things was just wrong.

In any case, we often play "The Name Game." The name for Mother and Father vary from culture to culture. The Nuclear Family consists of Mother, Father, Brother and Sister. In the Yanomamo tribe Buddy and Sissy (Brother and Sister) are not equally related to Mother and Father. Bi-linear means you are equally related and Uni-linear family means the family is in one line. Heritage through the father is Patrilineal and heritage through the mother in Matrilineal. Blood kinship or decent is consanguineal means related by blood. Affinal means marriage related, i.e. sister-in-law or daughter-in-law.

In the Yanomamo father is Fasi. Mother-Sister is Mosi. Mother-Brother is Mobr. Father's Brother is Fabr. The Uncle can be like a Father and the Aunt can be like a Mother in some societies. Cousins can be like brothers and sister.

Video Portrait of People: The Trobriand

This video takes place on the Trobriand Islands. Three are 28 islands. The Tobriand Islands are a 174-square-mile archipelago of coral atolls off the east coast of New Guinea. They are part of the nation of Papua New Guinea and are in Milne Bay Province. Most of the population of 12,000 indigenous inhabitants live on the main island of Kiriwina, which is also the location of the government station, Losuia. Other major islands in the group are Kaileuna, Vakuta, and Kitava. The group is considered to be an important tropical rainforest eco-region in need of conservation.

A Celebration of Life is what we are watching. Life depends on Yams. The men are responsible for the Yams. Banana and Coconut trees are privately owned. The culture says that it is more important to give than receive. Bundles of food is created and dried and then sold.

The women make money and do everyday tasks. In the Village of Kibwaga, the society is Matrilineal. It depends on the mother's line The chief's rule, but the women have the real power. The Yam House is a symbol of power. Wives provide economic strength. Some men may have nine or ten wives. There isn't much arguing among them.

Both fathers and mothers look after the kids. Beauty Magic is when they dress up to attract mates. At seven or eight years of age, Trobriand children begin to play erotic games with each other and imitate adult seductive attitudes. And four or five years later, at age 11 or 12 year old, they begin to pursue sexual partners. They change partners often. Women are just as assertive and dominant as men in pursuing or refusing a lover. This is not only allowed, but encouraged. The older adults sometimes step between teenagers and marriage if they don't like the match. Sexuality and mating is important during Harvest time.

The Trobriands believe that conception is the result of an ancestral spirit entering the woman's body. Even after a child is born, it is the mother's brother, not the father, who presents a harvest of yams to his sister so that her child will be fed with food from its own matrilineage, not the father's.

Missionaries introduced cricket and now the Villagers spends lots of time playing the game. It replaces their sexual games and the violent fighting that took place before mating. The men also have a single radio in the village. They gather around to listen.

A Widow and her Daughter sit and mourn the loss of the Husband and Father for months. The bundles they make show strength in the face of death. It takes her 3 days to make a skirt and sell it at Sagali Market. It will be an honor for another woman to wear the handmade skirt. The money she gets will go toward paying those who helped her care for her dead husband. Everyone in Mourning is paid. Those in morning shave their head and paint their faces black.

Kinship Continued

A **Clan** is *any uni-lineal kinship which is deep in genealogical depth and recognizes decent from a common mythological ancestor.* Matriclans is where ancestry is traced through the women's bloodline. Patrilineal is where the woman takes the man's name and the bloodline is traced through the man's ancestry. Exogamous is marrying outside the core group. Totemic is where the core group is named after nature. Ranked is ranking from top to bottom.

Origin Myths are tales or stories that go back to a cosmic time and account for the origin of people, animals and the natural world. Each group of people seeks to answer the questions: Where did I come from? Where am I going? Why am I here? And Why is ANYTHING here?

The book of Genesis in the Bible is Jewish, Christian and Muslim's creation story. We can trace our ancestry back to Adam and Eve and then their sons Cain and Abel. Cain is the Farmer who kills his brother Abel, who was a Shepherd. Cain goes with Abel's wife. Where did Abel's wife come from?

According to the Bible, or rather Arch Bishop Usher's interpretation of the Bible, the Earth was created in 4004 BC. Science tells us the Earth is 4.5 BILLION years old.

The Christian Creation Myth also tells us of three important Patriarchs Abraham, Jacob and Isaac. They are part of the 12 Tribes of Israel. The Bible Kinship story talks about Abraham and his wife Sarah. They hire Hagar, a Handmaiden from Egypt. They have a baby Ishmael. In Plural marriages there is a specific rank to the wives and their children. There may be jealousy between wives.

There is pain associated with memory. The bond between a mother and her children is strong. Matrifocal means that the focus of the culture is on mothers and child rearing.

1000 years ago no one had a last name. 500 years ago many people still didn't have last names. People were known by a first name and then either by where they lived or their occupation.

Currently our tribe is one that celebrates monogamy, but lots of native tribes practice polygamy. That means that they were not only able to have many mates, but were encouraged to do so. Polyandry is one male and many females. Polygyny is one women with lots of men.

In Tanzania (East Africa) the Kagura practice Exogamous Matrilineal Clans or Matriclans. Their tale of the Hyena and the Rabbit is an important Moral Lesson. Children aren't cut off in the Kagura society like ours are. The Hyena is the mother. The Mobr is the Mother's Brother. The Rabbit is the Trickster. During the Famine the Mother Hyenas kill the Rabbits. The Rabbit hides his mother so she won't be killed. No one is left to feed the Hyena. The Hyena dies and the Rabbit is left to hunt with mother. They live happily ever after. The Killing of Mothers is Matricide. The Killing of Sisters is Sororicidal. This is an instructional tale not to kill the women of the tribes or the tribe will die off like the Hyena

Similarly, Cain and Abel was also a cautionary tale about sibling rivalry. Murder is no solution to fighting over being father's favorite.

Sigmund Freud talks about the Oedipus Complex where the son lusts for the mother and kills the father. The Electra Complex is where daughters lust after fathers and kill their mothers. Polish Anthropologist **Bronisław Kasper Malinowski** wanted to be more famous than Freud even! Malinowski argued that Freud was wrong about family structures. He didn't think that sex was basis for authority and pointed toward Uncles and Aunts acting like Fathers and Mothers as an example. The Bifurcated Families Merge. This merger means Uncles and Aunts can't marry their nieces and nephews and that is a good thing.

In consanguineal kinship in anthropology, a parallel cousin or ortho-cousin is a cousin from a parent's same-sex sibling, while a cross-cousin is from a parent's opposite-sex sibling. Thus, a parallel cousin is the child of the father's brother (paternal uncle's child) or of the mother's sister (maternal aunt's child), while a cross-cousin is the child of the mother's brother (maternal uncle's child) or of the father's sister (paternal aunt's child). Where there are unilineal descent groups in a society matrilineal and/or Patrilineal), one's parallel cousins on one or both sides will belong to one's own descent group, while cross-cousins will not (assuming descent group exogamy).

Week 4: Variations in Subsistence Patterns

Papua New Guinea Movie

There are 700 Languages and some 30,000 people in Papua New Guinea. Papua New Guinea is an island in Indonesia. Half the island is Indonesian, the other half are the Papua. **Manus Island** is part of Manus Province in northern Papua New Guinea and is the largest of the Admiralty Islands. It is the fifth-largest island in Papua New Guinea.

Margaret Mead (December 16, 1901 – November 15, 1978) was a cultural anthropologist from American. She earned her bachelor's degree at **Barnard College** in **New York City** and her MA and PhD degrees from Columbia University. Mead served as President of the American Association for the Advancement of Science in 1975. She visited Manus in Papua New Guinea five times.

Coming of Age in Samoa is a book by Mead based upon her research and study of teenage girls – on the island of **Ta'u** in the Samoan Islands. The book details the sexual life of teenagers in Samoan society in the early 20th century, and theorizes that culture has a leading influence on psycho-sexual development. Margaret Mead had a great fondness for the people of Manus Island.

In Samoa or on Manus Island there is a village of fishermen. They use shells and dog teeth for money. They leave the islands in Outriggers to trade with other villages on other islands. Now the children leave for bigger cities on bigger islands. The Manus people have always lived off the sea and by the sea. They trade with gardeners and hunters.

Mead believed that a central part of Anthropology was honoring the people you study. She was not happy with the books based on other villages and people of the area. She saw that the West had dehumanized their relationships and way of life. Colonialism has left its mark and it isn't good.

Uiaku is the name of the main island. John Barker studied the tribes there for over a year and a half. In the 1960s Anthropology's aim was concerned with the connection between Colonialism and Anthropology. In the 1980s we see children in the village learning English, Math and History in School.

In the past John Baker took down old Folk Tales and wrote them down to preserve them. He noted 12 different clans and their histories. Each clan is separated by their morality. They are not supposed to talk about other people in other villages. When he asked questions about parents, grandparents and people in other villages, some of the people got angry.

The Village Council meets to make important decisions. They argued about the role of the anthologist. Some of them see the relationship as uneven. What do these people give us in return? They see the Anthropologist as rich. He should have a lot of things he can give them. So John Baker gives them a library of 250 books.

John Baker learned their language and made friends with them. He spent 2 to 3 years with them. He earned their respect.

Summary of Ongka's Big Moka

In the mid-1970's documentary film "Ongka's Big Moka" Ongka is the main character of the film. He is "one of most prominent leader or 'big man' of the Kawelka tribe" in the Western highlands, north of Mount Hagen in Papua New Guinea and trying to prepare the next moka (Ongka's Big Moka 1976). It is important to note that he is not the only 'big man' in his tribe (McDowell). Ongka's major opponent is Raima. Raima is also competing with Ongka on setting the date for the moka. Nearly ten years ago, Ongka's tribe (Kawelka) received moka from Peruwa, the 'big man' of another tribe in New Guinea, which mainly constituted of 400 pigs and other valuable and luxurious items in certain amounts. In the film, it was mentioned that it was common to include cows, shells, a truck car, a motorbike, and Australian Dollar in cash and cassowaries. Ongka wants not only to reciprocate the debt but also give an enormous (possibly the reason for naming the film as 'big' moka) gift with 600 pigs plus other valuable items and has been preparing it for almost five years.

Ongka has four wives and nine children. As illustrated in the film, Ongka has been married to his fourth wife, Riema, because she can help rear more pigs. One person can take care of 8 to 10 pigs at a time. His favorite wife is Rumbicore as she can take care up to 10 full-grown pigs. Moreover, Ongka needs the help of others in his tribe to be successful in the moka. However his position in his tribe is not as a commander but solely persuader. Thus a lot of effort, time and leadership skills or charisma seem to be required to achieve the 'big man' status. His speech-making skills throughout the film show how important it is to persuade people to work together.

By the time the filmmakers were to leave New Guinea, Ongka's big moka was postponed due to the accused sorcery to kill another tribe's Big Man. However, later Ongka managed to accomplish his moka with 600 pigs, 12 cassowaries, 8 cows, 10,000 Australian USD, a truck and a motorbike; the biggest moka ever given.

The Moka exchange takes place only when a particular tribe decides to give extra of what it has received from another tribe. The word moka can be described as "unreciprocated increment of a presentation, which brings prestige to the giver and also to exchanges which involve this kind of presentation" (Wagner 1415–1416). Therefore moka is practiced frequently as it brings unprecedented benefits to both the 'big man' and his tribe. The history of moka dates back to hundreds of years when tribes used moka for war reparations. Before the colonial periods (circa before the 1930s), the tribes or groups involved in fights came to terms to pay the costs of war in the forms of pigs and shells. In short, the obtained wealth was equal to the lost lives. If the relationship between tribes were to be improved for better, they would return the certain amounts of the reparations (Stewart and Strathern 125–134). In fact, it was the commencement of 'preparing moka' On the other hand, one member of Kawelka tribe says, "We used to fight and kill people. We didn't care. We killed them with spears and axes. Their people were angry, so we gave them pigs to make them feel better." Therefore, I think that in the case of Ongka's tribe, they have traditionally been engaged in moka to avoid conflicts and fights with other tribes. It is one of, if not the only, the means of maintaining peace by engaging in such diplomatic and economic relationships.

In order to understand the inclusion of pigs in moka in large numbers, the importance of pigs needs to be analyzed. Pigs are equivalent to money as local people have conceived it to be so for a long time and used to get wives and pay for troubles (in the film Ongka used pigs himself to compensate for the misunderstanding took place with the other tribe). Ongka says, "pigs are a strong thing. Pigs keep us going. You need pigs for everything […] if you don't have pigs, you are rubbish, you are nobody. There are no men who don't realize this." One can interpret that pigs have inherently been perceived not only as the source of food but also of prestige and wealth within the members of the tribe. Besides that, pigs are perhaps the most practical animals that one can invest whether individually or collectively.

The French sociologist Marcel Mauss, in his book The Gift, introduced one of the most prominent theories in the field of anthropology. He explained the importance of gift exchange and obligation to reciprocate. He argued that gift-giving is not altruistic; gifts are never truly free (Mauss 76). The obligation to give, to receive and to reciprocate exists in all range of societies in the form of social welfare in highly advanced social democracies (Mauss 71) or perhaps even in capitalism. Mauss' theory of gift exchange also emphasizes the gift economy and how it is distinctly different from commodity or barter economy. Gift economy or gift culture, by definition, is "a mode of exchange where valuables are not traded or sold but rather given without an explicit agreement for immediate or future rewards" (Cheal 1–19). As it is different from barter economy which underlines the immediate reciprocal and utility-based exchanges, moka chain is quite similar to the gift culture as it involves delayed reciprocity, obligation to reciprocate in order to maintain one's source of authority and wealth but also prevent any potential harm or conflicts on to their society as a whole. Another aspect of the gift theory on the spirit (hau) of the gift (taonga) that Mauss explains seems to play an important role among the highlanders in New Guinea. In the film, it was mentioned that during the moka giving ceremony, one person goes down to each pigs and their lineage (Ongka's Big Moka). I assume it is either because of their ancestral line playing a significant role in the value of pigs or presumably they do it so as to keep track of whether some particular pigs were gifted to them by the other tribe and reciprocate with the same, if not more, pigs of value. Nevertheless, Kawelka tribe values the notion of reciprocity, which is the belief in the spirit of the received gift in itself.

According to Emile Durkheim, the French sociologist, "A social fact is any way of acting, whether fixed or not, capable of exerting over the individual an external constraint; or: which is general over the whole of a given society whilst having an existence of its own, independent of its individual manifestations" (Durkheim 1895).

As moka is more than a mere transaction of pigs and other valuables, moka is about the economy, political and diplomatic relationships with other tribes. At the micro level, participating in moka brings prestige and honor to the individuals. Kawelka tribe accepts the moka as a structure of maintenance of their society in much wider scope. Therefore, moka exchange is one of the perfect examples of Durkheim's total social fact and proves to work just as well as the other societies that exist today.

Moka and kula exchanges have in common with the vitality of earning prestige and honor and keeping social relations with other member tribes. Two exchanges also use shells as a source of wealth or value. However, in kula exchange arm shells mainly passing regularly from west to east, and the necklaces from east to west, there seem to be no such strict rules in moka. Moreover, kula is about generosity while moka puts an important significance on the competition spirit between tribes to earn honor and put the receiver tribe in as much debt as possible so that they would never attack the donor tribe. Last but not least, the quantity seems to play a bigger part in moka rather than quality which is the case in

Moka is one of the perfect examples of the existence of gift culture which, Mauss argues, gives a whole insight into what it means to be human; the long-discussed question of anthropology.

Week 4: Midterm

Week 5: Socialization, Religion and Belief Systems

We think Halloween has always been there, but it hasn't. Irish Pagan beliefs mixed with American Protestant beliefs to create the modern Holiday as we know it.

Syncretism is the contact between two belief systems. Religious syncretism exhibits blending of two or more religious belief systems into a new system. It can also be the incorporation into a religious tradition of beliefs from unrelated traditions, which is different from polytheism.

The idea behind Halloween is that the dead aren't dead. There is a thin veil between to the two worlds and it lifted during the Harvest Season. Samhain is the Celtic Harvest Festival traditionally celebrated October 31st and All Saint's Day is the Catholic Holiday that follows on November 1st.

The Celts inhabited England and Ireland. They inhabited Gaul as well, but the Romans pushed them further West and North as they conquered Europe. They were seen as barbarians who lived in tribes. The Christianity the Romans brought with them mixed with the Ancient Druidism. The Celts worshiped nature and trees were sacred--particularly the Oak Tree. Caesar wanted to destroy the Pagan Religions and burned many of their Sacred Oaks.

Like Beltane, Samhain was seen as a special time, when the boundary between this world and the **Otherworld** could more easily be crossed. This meant the *Aos Sí*, the 'spirits' or **'fairies'**, could more easily come into our world. Most scholars see the *Aos Sí* as remnants of the pagan gods and nature spirits. At Samhain, it was believed that the *Aos S i* needed to be **propitiated** to ensure that the people and their livestock survived the winter. Offerings of food and drink were left outside for them. It was bad luck NOT to take care of the spirits. They could curse you. The souls of the dead were thought to revisit their homes seeking a safe place to rest. Feasts were had, where the souls of dead family members were beckoned to attend and a place set at the table for them.

Mumming and dressing up in costume was part of the festival. It involved people going door-to-door in costume (or in disguise), often reciting verses in exchange for food. The costumes may have been a way of imitating, and disguising oneself from the fair folk.

Christian Missionaries tried to convince the Celts that Halloween was bad or evil. It is thought they created All Saints day to give the Celts an Alternative Holiday to Celebrate instead of Halloween. The Catholics believed that souls wait in Limbo or Purgatory. Prayers have to be said for the dead or they can't move on to Heaven or Hell. Catholics believe in a wall or gate keeping people on the other side. They didn't believe in reincarnation and they couldn't explain a person's fortune or misfortune. Heaven and Hell are considered reward and punishment in place of Karma.

This conversion of Pagan myths is also found in the Legend of King Arthur. It is likely Arthur was a Roman Solider who became King when he united England's Pagan Tribes. Many of the Arthurian Legends have roots in Celtic Mythology.

We turned out discussion to Horror Movies. Some of the Horror movies mentioned by classmates included: *Halloween, Friday the 13th, Nightbreed, The Lady In White, Shock Them Dead, Flatliners, Pet Cemetery, Candyman, Hideaway*. There are also classics like *Dracula* and *Frankenstein*. Why do we watch Horror Movies and celebrate them on Halloween? We watch them because they provide excitement and terror. They provide a rush. People have a fascination with death and some people get a thrill out of watching people in agony.

The Motif or Theme of many Horror Movies is Death, Life, Resurrection and an inability to Kill Evil. Where does Evil live? Inside of Us? Outside of Us? Maybe both? These movies ask questions about human nature and our world view. A lot of cultures deal with these important questions without the aid of Horror movies. The Horror novels and movies help us deal with these things here in America.

We have forgotten the idea of Zoroastrianism, where light and dark are forever battling each other. These ancient ideas have found their way into our most modern folk tales--aka Horror Movies.

Week 6: Politics ad Law in Comparative Perspective

Politics comes from the Greek word *Polis*, which means City. The suffix *"ics"* means affairs of. Politics has to do with the affairs of the City. David Easton wrote an article in 1959 on Political Anthropology. *"Politics is that aspect of society which makes binding decisions for a society or its subdivisions."* Easton talked about a Regime or a way in which political power is distributed. Regime refers to the Rules of the Game.

Part of Politics is the presence of a Leader. There are lots of ways to get people to do what you want them to. The easiest way to do this is through physical force. The Mafia and Military use physical force. Even parents can use physical force to get kids to do things. But who has the right use this physical force? It has to be socially sanctioned.

Leaders are often described as Charismatic. Charisma is the Greek word for Gift of Grace. Another source of Authority is Patrilineal. Power is passed down from father to son. There is also authority by Bureaucracy or Ruling By Desks. Decisions in Democracy are often not Democratic. People are supposed to have a voice, but are often influenced by parties, etc. Government is Autocratic by its very nature. Students at OSU really don't have much power over the politics and polices of OSU. It is State run institution that has a very formal hierarchy. Native Tribes like the Yanomamo don't have a State or formal Government.

Political Culture is a Culture of Symbols. The USA uses flags, jets, donkeys, elephants and the white house. Spin Doctors and Speech Writers create and use these symbols. They use them with the Family Values platform, among other things.

Politics were emotionally loaded during the Vietnam War. This was reflected in the music, clothes and counterculture of the time. There was a split in what Americans believed we were all about. There was no agreement on a single symbol. The war in Vietnam was a symbol of the war going on at home with Civil Rights, etc.

The mood shifted with the Gulf War in 1991. There was talk of fighting for liberty and being patriotic. Words like God, Sacrifice and Flag were thrown around a lot during Desert Storm.

Why were we even in Vietnam? Were we fighting over Rice or

over Communism? It was never very clear what the objective was. We never really won that war. America's pride was hurt. There was talking of nuking them and ending the war like we did in Japan. But there was a great deal of fear that Russia and China would drop a nuclear bomb on us in retaliation and no one wanted the possible Apocalypse that would result from that.

We might not have ever been involved in any conflicts in the Pacific or in Asia, except Japan bombed Pearl Harbor in 1942. Japan was attacking China and other parts of Asia as well. We figured the enemy of our enemy is our friend. We had stakes in the future of Korea and Vietnam. At the end of World War II we saw Communism split Europe and Asia. Germany was divided. Korea and Vietnam both ended up being divided in to North and South.

The Viet Minh and Ho-Chi Minh and Giap were all Communist and they used Gorilla Warfare in their countries. The French had colonies in Vietnam and we agreed to help France in their struggles to maintain control. We were also dedicated to preventing the spread of Communism. We weren't able to do anything about the Communist Revolution in China in 1949, but we could promise to help the French against the Ho-Chi Min. This was the start of the US being involved in "brush fires."

Korea was bigger and better organized than Vietnam. Some 50 countries were there, not just the US. We were almost defeated in Korea. We were pushed back to the ocean, in fact. It was 46 French to every 54 Viet Minh. The Battle of Dien Bien Phu was the Waterloo battle for Korea. In the spring of 1954 the French were badly beaten. Defeat seemed inevitable. They were trapped in a bowl shaped valley in the mountains. The Ho-Chi Min won.

There was a Peace Conference in Geneva. The big powers and little powers talked. They made a decision to divide up Vietnam between the North and South. In 1956 elections were held and they were supposed to be reunited. Eisenhower didn't sign the peace talk agreements. The US didn't want a Communist or Ho-Chi Min leader. The Republic in South Vietnam rallied. Voi Dehem was not popular there. He had been the second in command during the Japanese invasion. He was assassinated in 1961.

The US equipped and trained the Vietnamese army under ARVN. The ARVN's couldn't fight. The Communist grew their support and the South and was threatening to take over. There was a secret or quiet war from 1954 until 1960.

Kennedy was elected and used Counter-Insurgency tactics. He had the Green Berets out-gorilla the gorillas. In 1961 we sent the first of 10,000 troops. The number grew to 20,000 and then to 40,000 by 1963. In 1964 10,000 Marines were sent. It was a lot of man power. Then JFK wanted out of the war. It was not going our way. It wasn't working. Vietnam was going to have to be left to fight itself. The CIA was making lots of money off the war and didn't want it to end. Was JKF killed because he wanted to end the war? Some think so.

Lyndon Johnson took Kennedy's place after he was shot. Almost immediately he declared that he wouldn't be the first President to lose a war. In 1967 there were over 500,000 troops there. 58,000 men were killed in Vietnam and 260,000 wounded. The amount wounded is about half the population of Columbus, Ohio!

Vietnam ripped our culture in half. There were many protests on college campuses, but perhaps the most famous is the Kent State Shootings. There were riots at the main campus of OSU too. Guards had to control the gates on Neal Avenue. A lot of people got beat up or sent to jail.

What did the movement accomplish or fail to accomplish? The movement against Vietnam did manage to end the draft. It lowered the voting age to 18 instead of 21. It also ended the war eventually.

Vietnam Movie

Summer of 1964 Gulf of Tonkin Resolution came, but it was NOT a declaration of war. A destroyer escorted a Maddox Patrol. It was an International Warship in enemy waters. Where international and Vietnam waters met is where it crossed the line. The ship was carrying out a spy mission. They weren't under actual attack. A weather pattern on the radar was mistaken for an attack. Johnson ignored this fact when it was revealed to him later. He voted to go to war. 560,000 troops were sent over.

The Hill is the story of tree men, two of whom were sergeants, who became friends. JC was married and had a family. Bruce was a college dropout whose jail sentence was to serve in the war. JC had been drafted. On November 30, 1967 the made an advance in Vietnam. There were 114 men in Patrol and 16 Platoons.

The three men spent 8 to 10 days walking in the Jungle. Jimi Hendrix's song "Grizzly" was about the Vietnam War and that moment in time. The Helicopter had scouted ahead and found where the troops needed to go. A landing zone is cut out of the jungle so the Helicopter can land and drop off supplies to the troops. One solider is hit by a falling tree. David Foye is the Commanding Officer. There is artillery and airstrikes throughout the night.

The next night the patrol covers Hill number 943. They are ambushed when they reach the top. ALPHA company takes some casualties. Alpha company waits for airstrikes. They shoot in the dark, but can't see who they are shooting at. Two men are wounded in the ambush and one man died. More men are wounded in the effort to shoot the enemy. There is a total of 13 wounded, including one civilian, one Sergeants and two enlisted. Shrapnel went everywhere. That accident delayed the advance by 10 minutes.

After 3 days of fighting, the US takes the Hill back. The enemy withdrew from Hill 943. It was three days after Christmas when the enemy retreated. JC and Bruce were wounded in the fight. Jim, the third man, was killed. Body counts are difficult to determine at the end of the fighting. A body count is just numbers. The real toll is emotional.

Week 7: Ethnicity and Racism in Perspective

Bosnia has been in the News. The **Bosnian War** is an international armed conflict that took place in Herzegovina and Bosnia between 1992 and 1995. Following a number of violent incidents in early 1992, the war is commonly viewed as having started on April 6, 1992. The war was part of the breakup of Yugoslavia. Yugoslavia is connected and divided by Language. The Ottoman Turks took over the area from 1490 until 1914. So we had the Muslims vs. Christian Turks.

Anyway, after the Slovenian and Croatian secession from the **Socialist Federal Republic of Yugoslavia** in 1991, the multi-ethnic Socialist Republic of Bosnia and Herzegovina, which was inhabited by mainly **Muslim Bosniaks** (44 percent), as well as Orthodox **Serbs** (32.5 percent) and Catholic **Croats** (17 percent) declared their Independence in February 1992. The political representatives of the Bosnian Serbs, who had boycotted the declaration, rejected this. Following Bosnia and Herzegovina's declaration of independence war broke out.

The conflict was initially between the Yugoslav Army units in

Bosnia which later transformed into the Army of Republika
Srpska (VRS) on the one side, and the Army of the Republic of
Bosnia and Herzegovina (ARBiH) which was largely composed of
Bosniaks, and the Croat forces in the Croatian Defense Council
(HVO) on the other side. Tensions between Croats and Bosniaks
increased throughout late 1992, resulting in the Croat–Bosniak
War that escalated in early 1993. The Bosnian War was characterized
by bitter fighting, indiscriminate shelling of cities and towns, ethnic
cleansing and systematic mass rape, mainly perpetrated by Serb and
to a lesser extent, Croat and Bosniak forces. Events such as the Siege
of Sarajevo and the Srebrenica massacre later became iconic of the
conflict.

The Serbs committed genocide for political, ethical and religious
reasons. The UN and US felt like they had a moral obligation to
intercede. A reporter from Christian Science Monitor was missing.
The US wanted to prevent WWIII. Serbs killed 40-60 thousand
people because they didn't like their ethnicity. The Serbs had ethnic
pride and wanted political power.

Week 8: Japanese History and Culture

Japan has four major islands from North to South: Hokkaido,
Honshu, Shikoku, and Kyushu. The total land mass is about the size
of Montana and California. Japan has around 120 Million people in a
very concentrated area. Compare that to 250 Million in the US in a
much larger area. People don't have much personal space. However,
the crime rate is quite low. There are more murders in Columbus
than there are in Tokyo.

Japan has the most active volcanoes in the world. There is a spine
of mountains that runs through Japan. Japan is isolated. The islands
of Japan don't have very many natural resources. They have had to
import most of what they have needed.

Japan was influenced by China. They borrowed their writing or
alphabet from the China. The Japanese have over 2000 characters in
their alphabet. One has to know over 1500 characters just to read a
newspaper. They began growing rice only after Korean invaders
came in 300 BC.

In any case, Japan has had the longest continuous dynasty or
monarchy. It begins with Jim-mu Teno. The Imatos came to power.
The family was transformed into demigods or Amaterasu Kami

Sama. They were elevated to god-level. No one is sure where the Japanese came from. The Ainu were the aboriginal inhabitants. Modern Japanese people came from Polynesia or China or somewhere. Japan is often lumped together with the rest of Asia. Asia includes: Malaysia, Indonesia, India, Thailand, Philippians, Manchuria, China, Burma, Japan, Korea and Vietnam.

In any case Japan has a specific Hierarchy: Emperor, Shogun, Daimyo, Samurai, Peasants, Artisans and Outcasts. The Position of the Emperor was split from the Warrior role. In 1192 Minamoto declares himself a Shogun. It was kind of like he knighted himself. Ninjas were assassins who worked outside of society. They had a lot of tricks, but they were not mystical.

Westerners reached Japan and Japan didn't like the chaos they brought. Eventually they closed themselves off from the West. Westerners were banned from Japan from the 1600s until 1868. The Meiji Restoration began a slow movement toward opening up from 1853 until 1868. Then there were peasant rebellions. Eventually, Japan opened up to the west due to whale oil. American Whalers were being killed. We needed to be friends with Japan. We needed each other's resources. We had an uneasy relationship with them until WWII. Then they became enemies.

We bombed the hell out of them. Japan lost a lot of men, partially because to die for the Emperor was a great honor. That is reason for Kamikaze Pilots. (Kamikaze translates to God-Wind.) The group has always been more important to the Japanese than the individual. And we see this not only in war, but in the way they approach business in modern times. Anyway, the Gruta Canal was the turning point of the Japanese war on land. They were basically defeated when we dropped the atomic bomb on Hiroshima and Nagasaki.

Japanese Religion

Most religions are more concerned with the afterlife than pre-life. Fear of the Future is what occupies the minds of most. Reincarnation deals with Pre-Life and the idea of Reincarnation is found in Hinduism and Buddhism in Asia. Cosmology is the idea of exploration for universe based on religion. Today we focus on Science. Science and Religion blend sometimes. There are a dazzling array of religions and views in the world. Japanese Shinto is one of many religions.

Shintoism includes the idea of animism. Animism is one of the oldest beliefs. It is the idea that all people, animals and objects have life. There are many sacred places around us. These sacred places were often marked with Torii Gates. The Gates are where the Light or the God Kami can come through. God is a divine spirit that exists but it is an energy. There are other Gods and Goddesses attached to Shintoism, not just Kami. There is also no guilt or sin or any of the other issues attached to Christianity. (McLeod has a Sun Goddess House in his Office to Honor the Shinto Goddess.)

Polytheism is the belief in many gods. Izanami of and Izanagi are part of the Creation Myth. They stuck a staff into the sea and swirled it around. A sword came out and landed where Japan was formed. The islands were created by this sword that fell from the ocean. Amaterasu has the sun, but the gods anger her. She hides it in a cave. The gods beg her to come out and she does.

Monotheism is the belief in a single god. In Japan they believe in Shintoism, but Buddhism is a big part of their culture. Buddhism began in India and traveled through Korea and China to get to Japan in the 6th Century. Buddhism also includes the idea of Karma. There is a balance of justice and left over issues from one life follow one into the next life.

Japan has been exposed to Christianity, but it did not take hold in that country like it did other places. Christians are currently a minority in Japan. However, Christians did manage to destroy the idea of Animism in many other places around the world. For example, the ancient Celts believed in Animism, but the Christians stamped that out of them.

In Shintoism the color of death is white, not black. There is no hell or afterlife. They have a cleansing ritual for the dead before they are burned. 1600 years ago they had key shaped tombs. Now there are Torii gates. Shintoism is more embedded into Japanese Culture than an actual religion.

Other than birth, death and marriage rituals, there isn't much to do. They don't have churches, but temples. There are no Popes, Bishops, Cardinals or Priests like Catholics. There is no hierarchy of people in charge. It is private and family oriented. There are 70,000 to 100,000 temples for people to visit, which are connected in a loose confederation. Usually a family will live near a temple and use the one their ancestors used for hundreds of years. The Meiji Shrine has some 600 arches and worth billions of dollars, but doesn't belong to any single person or anything.

Taoism is the idea of alternating opposites: Light and Dark, Good and Evil, Male and Female. They are a part of one another. You can have one without the other. That also applies to needing the West to define the East. Bushido is another important concept. It means the way of the warrior. This was the way of the ancient Samurai.

Movie On Japan

Japan is the Golden Island. There were volcanic eruptions that created the rich soil now there. Rice fields cover land that now. Once again a volcano erupts and covers the orange trees in ash. Kids wear helmets to protect themselves from falling ash and debris. The Japanese are under the constant threat of earthquakes and volcano eruptions. They have learned to be prepared for disasters and adapt to changes quickly because of where they live.

At the temple we see a monk praying or meditation. Just a few miles away from the ancient temple are factories reminding him of the thriving Japanese Economy.

Work begins at 8am. A girl who is 20 years old has been working there since she was 7 years old. She is taking a business course to get a promotion. It is her parent's farm. Her have been farming the rice terraces for generations. The family has since added orange trees to their farm. Parents, Grandparents and Children are all under one roof.

The average Rice Farmers have a long life of hard labor. During Winter they bring in new soil for the fields that have depleted soil levels. When Spring comes they prepare the new soil for planting Mud and seeds are scattered. Young plants bud in the field. Only women have the job of picking the rice. During the summer there are storms and flooding. Sometimes there are high winds. The hard work required in the field shapes Japanese Culture and Personality.

The sister of the girl who works on the farm works in the factory nearby has a phone, TV, VCR and clothes. She is saving to go to Disneyland. The girl goes with her grandfather to a Shinto Shrine. They pray for successful harvest and for her brother to pass his college entry exam.

The movie shows the Torii gates in front of the shrine. The narrator talks about the dances and rituals performed by the tombs and shrines. Shinto means "the way of the gods." The Gods are everywhere, the trees and water, etc There are festivals and rituals that everyone takes part in even if Shinto isn't something they give much thought to.

The Japanese love bathing. Bathers soak themselves outside of the bath first. Then they get in. The public baths give them a sense of community. Same sex shares the public baths now, but it didn't used to be that way.

Buddhism bloomed in Japan. It came from India, Korea and China. Shinto is concerned with the living, while Buddhism addresses the afterlife or pre-life. Shintoism and Buddhism complement each other.

Japan has a focus on the Arts. They also focus on poetry and novels. The Japanese borrowed their alphabet from China. But the symbols are completely different. You need to know 1850 characters in Japanese just to read a newspaper in Japan. Literacy takes up a lot of time in school. Japan has a higher literacy rate than Western Countries.

Back to the Farm. In the hamlet of Macedo there are 16 farms. There are three generations under each roof in town. The eldest son will take over. Rice is a staple part of the Japanese Diet. Now their diets have a lot more variety in them. There is a meeting of families in the hamlet. Both sexes are present and able to speak up. There is a unanimous decision to clean the channels for irrigation. Rice cultivation requires a large amount of water. The whole community will help the project.

In each family house there is a shrine. Under the shrine is are all the family documents. There is a list of ancestors and favors done or owed. If one person can't pay a debt, the family will be responsible for paying the debt as soon as they can.

Second Movie on Japan

Why did the Japanese bomb Pearl Harbor? Millions of Japanese died during WWII. There is a shrine to them. There was much political controversy over the shrine. Yasho Hero Nashani is the Prime Minister. He talks about how the Japanese are searching for a place in the world.

In the 1930s Japan wanted to expand their empire. They expanded into China a bit. They spread a great deal of propaganda. Japan took over Manchuria. They wanted to be like England in

India, but the world looked at their expansion as negative. The West was pressing for an oil embargo. Japan needed oil, which is part of the reason they attacked both China and the US.

After they lost in WWII, they needed economic help. MacArthur distributed land to the peasants. Women got the right to vote. Industrial Cartels were broken up. Japanese recovery was slow. Japan was been colonized by England, Russia, France and the Netherlands. They took lots of land around the mainland of Japan.

They have many factories today from Heavy Industry to High Tech. They produce media, software and textiles or fashion. They have high quality items and attention to detail. Despite the great products they produce, the factories are no better than those in the third world. Women in particular have problems with working in the factories.

In school only girls study home economics. The middle class has made progress over all, but women have been encouraged to become wives and mothers still. The males are the ones graduating college and getting the top jobs. Women do work, but often just part time. They are often seen as secondary like immigrant labor in the US.

Wives will play tennis and men will play golf. The children will take swimming lessons. The man will hand over his paycheck and women make the budget for the family. Women are growing in power in Japan though. Advertisers want to get their input. They are competing with men for better jobs.

Home Movies from 1959 Japan

McLeod visited Japan in 1959 with his family. He returned in 1983 and it had changed a great deal in the 20 plus years between visits. We see a girl dressed for a Shinto Holiday. McLeod tells us about his father who was in the Air Force. When McLeod Senior was in Air Force he was stationed in Japan, which is why our teacher got to go. The home movie shows a cross and a Christian church. McLeod explains that Christianity is rare in Japan.

The Japanese love to celebrate Western Holidays like Halloween and Christmas even if most of them are not Christian. He shows us a picture of Shinto Shrine and Torii. We also see some farmers racing their bikes.

McLeod talked about how the Minnesota State University has a special program where you can go to their college in Japan. You can get in-state fees if you come from the USA. Akita Japan is where it is located. Classes are taught in English even though 90% of the student body is Japanese. You can begin your instruction in Japan and transfer to American to finish. There are six levels of English and then General Education Curriculum. Americans can take four levels of Japanese.

McLeod coached football at Minnesota State University. The dining hall offers mostly Japanese dishes. Japanese and Americans share dorm rooms. Japanese guys love blonds. JET Programs refer to Japanese English Training.

Week 9: Final

Citizens of the World: We are all Citizens of the Earth. Our culture is not just limited to a city, state or country. Very few people are isolated and so every culture affects other cultures. Especially today, where no place is unreachable and news travels faster than ever before. This class was supposed to be a window in the world through various cultures.

The Industrial Revolution changed all of civilizations from small to large. The move from an Agricultural to Industrial was not a smooth or even transition. Civilized Countries or First World Countries are ones like the US, England and Australia. Secondary Civilizations or World include Communist Countries like Russia. They have industry, but things still aren't great. Third World Countries are poor with little to no industry and very poor living countries. The world's wealth is distributed unevenly. The Northern Countries are rich and the Southern Countries are poor.

Some countries import more than the export, while others export more than import. Those who export make the most money.

We take for granted things like clean drinking water, four walls and a roof to live in as well as electricity. 1.7% of US budget goes to foreign aid to help 3rd World Countries. Democracy really depends on the education of the citizens.

There will be questions from each chapter. There will be only one question about Ethnicity. There will be a lot of questions about Politics. Be prepared to Detail Aspects of Religion. There will be six questions on Vietnam.

Russia: That We Are Friends

As my second assignment, I picked to write on the *Now That We are Friends* lecture. It connected more with the films than the others. I went to the Conference on American Identity on October 4th to listen to Dr. G Yarovoy, Dr. A Nechayev and Ms. Shumkova. They discussed, "*Russian Perspective on America.*"

It is always difficult to know how to handle relations after the Berlin Wall came down and the Soviet Union Crumbled. Neither side really knows who is their friend or enemy and this makes trust difficult. America had many misconceptions about Russia and Russia had many misconceptions about America. This first speech was an effort to dispel these misconceptions.

Russia, I began to see, was not so different from America in the past. America modernized and Russia did not, so visiting there would be like traveling back in time. Anyway, Capitalism is slowing taking hold—especially where the Universities are concerned. Although it is common to hear about the big industries in Moscow, it is unusual to hear about the industries in Samara.

In the Second Speech the situation was looked at more widely. It was interesting to hear how America was like forbidden fruit to them. America was the Golden Dream to Russians like California was the Golden Dream to me. When I visited California this summer, I realized that my dream wasn't realistic. I think it has been like that for Russians. They were disappointed in the reality of America. The speaker has realized that Capitalism isn't necessarily a good thing. He sees the potential evils or problems with Capitalism.

I like the lecture and found the compare and contrast portions particularly interesting. We are both huge countries and world powers. Perhaps we can view each other as Sisters in the Global Community now. I agree that America and Russia should learn to work together.

Elements of Japanese Culture
Japanese 231

Instructor: Jennifer Dell-Ernstrom
Meetings: Monday thru Thursday 1:40 to 2:40pm
Winter 1996

Course Description: The First Half of the course focuses on major themes and aesthetics in Japanese History. The Second Half concentrates on the major elements of contemporary Japanese Culture. Material will be be presented through readings.

Materials: Edwin O Reischauer and Marius B Jansen. *The Japanese Today: Change and Continuity*, 199
H Paul Varley, *Japanese Culture*, 1984. Third Edition

January 2, 1996 Geography and Natural Resources

Hokkaido is the Northern Most Island of Japan It is the least populated part of Japan and wasn't settled really until the 1800s. The Climate is like Ohio and they get snow. The Southern Island is the main island. Our teacher Jennifer Dell-Ernstrom visited Hokkaido for a summer when she was just 16 years old. She graduated and was in Sapporo, Japan for a year. After that she went to work for Sony in New York. Later she worked for Japanese Security Agency in Boston, where she was a consultant. She got her Masters in Japanese from Harvard with a particular interest in Japanese Literature. She is also very interested in Buddhism.

The Main Island is known as Honshu. The Capital of Japan is Tokyo. Other cities include: Kobe, Osaka, Shikoku, Kyushu, Nagasaki and Historical Kyoto. Ryukyu Islands are 400 miles South. There are some 78 islands, but only 48 are inhabited. Okinawa Island is now a US Military Base.

Lots of land in Japan is uninhabitable due to steep mountain ranges. It is half the size of England, but bigger than Italy still. There are currently about 124 Million people in Japan. Hong Kong and Singapore have a Higher Density. For comparison Boston has 1.5 Million, New York has 8 ½ Million and Columbus has less than 1 Million. Tokyo has 27 Million people. Sapporo has 2 Million. Kyoto has 1.5 Million and Osaka has 16.5 Million.

US and Japan have sister cities. Saitama (which is near Tokyo) is Mansfield's Sister City.

The Climate of Japan ranges from Upstate New York to Florida. Only the Southern Islands are Tropical-like. The rainy season is June. They have a 260 day farming season. Typhoons are a danger in late summer and early fall. Some houses have no insulation or central heat. They have electric carpet, which is similar to an Electric Blanket. Fuel is expensive. There is little air conditioning as well.

Japan doesn't have a lot of natural resources. There are a lot of forests and mountains, but not a lot of fresh water. The Lumber Industry has done well. They import woods to US, Great Britain and much of Europe. They were able to cultivate and farm both fish and seaweed. The whaling industry is big in Japan. The meat is rubbery and oily, but considered a delicacy there. They only produce a small amount of coal. Most of what they use is imported. They also have to import copper, lead, iron, petroleum and oil. They used to produce cotton and silk in the early years, but they don't any more.

The exchange rate is 102 Yen to 1 American Dollar. It used to be 240 Yen to 1 American Dollar. The Yen is getting stronger. The American Dollar is getting weaker. Japanese Economy is is flux because of competition and low confidence in the Yen. On the upside, it is a good market for Teachers from America to go over to Japan and Teach English, etc.

Other odds and ends: Japan is known as The Land of Rising Sun. When they write their name, it is usually last name first to show respect. And they will add San which is similar to Mr. or Mrs. The Japanese Language uses characters similar to Chinese. The characters are called Kanji. They use two different sylibarus or alphabets. Hiragana are Native Japanese Words. Katakana are foreign words that are borrowed. An example of Katakana would be Hambaga for Hamburger or Wopo for Word Processor. Japanese has fewer sounds than English. L, R and Th are missing. The English have inflection when speaking, but the Japanese are flat when speaking. The Chinese have 3 different tones.

January 8, 1996 Pre-History and Early History

Jomon was the Stone Age Period in Japan. It was from 8,000 BC to 300 BC. Yayoi was the Bronze Age in Japan. It was from 300 BC to 300 AD. Kofun was the Tomb Period, which was 300 AD to 600 AD. China and other countries were more advanced than Japan during the Stone Age. Pottery, Bracelets, and Earrings were found at Archaeological Sites. The people who lived in Japan during this time were Hunters and Gathers. Not much is really known other than the Pottery was used for Rituals.

People of the Stone Age were conquered by mainlanders. The Native Ainu were pushed up North. The Ainu looked like Native Americans—slightly Caucasian. Most have intermarried and are more a memory than a pure racial group. They had no written language and have been losing the memory of the spoken word.

The Jomon people became the Yoyoi people. It seems that people from Japan interacted from people from China. They weren't exactly conquered. Bronze and Iron Technology came in the 3rd Century BC. They gained the ability to elevate the fields. It became the agriculture standard and overall standard of living increased.

Pottery changed. The Potter's wheel were used and they were able to make smooth sides. They made tableware, goblets and cups. The Pottery alternated between smooth and zigzag design. Some pots only had a single band around them for a decoration.

Burials were important—particularly of important people. Swords from China were often found at Burial Sites. Dotaku is a bell with 12 sides. They created a sort of Calendar with the Bell. Mirrors were made and considered to have supernatural power. The early tombs showed a people who didn't fight much and valued family.

The Chinese Writing Chronicled the People of Yayoi. The Chinese called them Wa, which meant Dwarfed or Stunted. They believed that Japan was split up into many tiny countries. The people of Japan sent a mission to the Mainland China and wrote about it. The Chinese also wrote about the Japanese coming to their territory.

The Queen Consolidated power and ruled with Authority. They believed she came from the Gods and had magical powers. She was a mediator from the Gods. It wasn't clear how large of an area in Japan she ruled. Her named was Himiko or Pimiko. This, among other things, suggested a matrilineal lineage in Japan. At least it was once that way—not so much anymore. This period of time saw people beginning to divide into social classes. This is also beginning of Art in Japan. Art was not fancy at the time, but simple and natural. Mirrors, swords and jewels were important items during this time.

The Tomb Period saw the Japanese Population grow into the

Thousands. The Kingdom stretched from the Southern Islands to Northern Most Island. They built impressive tombs in toward the end of the period—hence the name. The Tombs were built near water for the Emperors. It took hundreds of people many days, weeks and months to build the tombs.

The Kingdom had an army during this time. They fought more frequently. They buried horses in the tombs along with the Emperors and his weapons. Haniwa were cylinders outside of the tomb. They took on different shapes—often being shaped like people. By the 6th Century they took on the shapes of animals as well.

Was Japan invaded during this time? They suddenly had horses and riding warriors. The tombs near water suggested the the Japanese had rulers that were from some other place during the Tomb Period. Japan also had Military Outposts in Korea. They had changed from the people of the Bronze Age. The tribal groups of Japan had been known as the Uji. The Emperor was only slightly higher than his people. His position was symbolic in many ways.

Experts aren't sure where Shinto came in. The Japanese may have always worshiped nature. But it wasn't until the Tomb Period that they began worshiping their ancestors. The name Shinto means *"Way of the Gods."* Kami means God, Divine or Spirit. In Principle, Shinto is about how humans, animals and nature are connected. Everything should inspire awe. Kami is used in Matsuri or a Portable Shrine. Matsuri is a very important Festival in Shinto. It began as a way to celebrate both planting and harvesting. Now there are games and food at the festivals.

Shinto doesn't have any idea about death. It is all about life. It is about being present in the here and now. Kami is beneficial and kind. The divine ones are rarely bad or mean. Shinto doesn't really have code of ethics though. If murder is committed it is a part of life. There is no shame or blame. They do have purification rituals, which are very important though. A Shinto Shrine will have an external fountain with tin cups so that you can wash your hands and rinse your mouth.

Shinto has a rich Mythology—including a Creation Myth. It came about around the 7th Century. It deals with Chaos and the idea of Yin and Yang. Darkness sank down and Light rose. Siblings deities were created a drifting land. A spear is pulled out and the drips form the island of Japan. This created many other gods. The Sun Goddess ruled over the heavens. Her grandson gave sacred regalia—jewels, mirrors and sword. The great grandson became the Emperor of Japan. Myth was written down in 700AD. It was written down as true history.

The First known book was Record of Ancient Matter or The Kojiki. It was written in 712 and was similar to the Bible. The other book was written about 720. History was recorded, but much of it is actually mythology. It was written in Chinese, not Japanese though.

The most important shrine is ISE. The House image is of the Sun Goddess in a Mirror. It is the National Shrine and the Ancestral Shrine of the Imperial Family. It is made of unpainted Cyprus. It is really, really, really old. It is maintained and refurbished every 20 years.

A Torii is a Gateway Shrine. The function of a *torii* is to mark the entrance to a sacred space. They come in all sizes and are painted red. The most famous one is at Jimia and in the water.

January 9, 1996 Nara Period History and Culture

Japan's capitol city was wherever the court was. It often moved from city to city. In Shinto the place where the Emperor died was considered impure. Shinto was all about purity.

Shinto was in Japan for a long time, but then Buddhism came to the country around 552 via Korea. Foreigners came to Japan and brought Buddhism. it is estimated that around 1/3 of the Aristocrats in Japan were from other countries. Shinto Kami wasn't competitive, so it blended nicely.

Both Buddhism and Shinto existed side by side. There wasn't a conflict since they complimented each other. Shinto dealt with life and Buddhism dealt with the afterlife. Marriage and Birth are still celebrated in Shinto Ceremonies. Buddhism comes in when there are funerals. Buddhism also appealed because of the art. It was a very civilized religion.

Buddhism began in India a thousand years before the Nara Period. It began with the teachings of Gautama around 500BC. His teachings spread throughout India out into Asia—i.e. China and Korea. Siddhartha Gautama taught about cycles and reincarnation. Life was painful and the best way to escape suffering was to follow The 8 Fold Path. It was important to have the right job, right concentration, right speech and right intentions. Reaching Enlightenment was only possible for a few—monks and nuns mostly.

Buddhism split into Liberal Greater Vehicle Mahayana and Conservative Lesser Vehicle Hinayana. The older type of Buddhism was limited only to the Higher Class of people. The only art able to be produced was religious. The peasants thought it was all rather magical at first. But they eventually latched onto the idea of learning to no longer suffer. Then Buddhism became for everyone. The new type of Buddhism entered Japan. Liberal Mahayana believed that everyone was capable of reaching Nirvana. They believed in a Bodhisattva or Buddha to Be, an Enlightened Teacher or Yoda-like person. There are two forms of Buddha—the human and the god. The God is not a deity, but a universal energy. Transcendent Buddhism is about manifestations.

Japanese Confucianism was also big in the Nara Period. Feudalism dominated the country. Confucius spoke to the idea of having Ethics and being in Public Service.

Prince Shoktokia wanted Buddhism in Japan and texts to be written in Japanese. He was the Empress's right hand man. He was a scholar who was well read and who wrote Japan's first Constitution. It was general and vague, but it embodied Confucius and Buddha both. He believed the government should be ethical, etc. It was an important document that assured the Japanese freedom. It referred to Japan as the Land of the Rising Sun and China as the Land of the Setting Sun. He wanted Japan to be an equal to China. There was intense interaction between China and Japan during this time.

Many Reforms happened during this time. They wanted to nationalize all Agricultural Lands. The Lands belonged to the Emperor and were merely worked upon by the people. The Reform was supposed to make it more equal. This was based on Confucius's ideas. It was difficult to enforce though with no real bureaucracy in place.

All Providences needed officials and then with the implementation of the officials it became easier to rule. It was a Taino Bureaucracy. They relied on the Chinese language. Nara was built in Chinese Checkerboard fashion. There was a system of court ranking rather than ruling families. A Ronin was an Emperor-less Samurai.

The samurai (or bushi) were the warriors of premodern Japan. They later made up the ruling military class that eventually became the highest-ranking social caste of the Edo Period (1603-1867).

Samurai employed a range of weapons such as bows and arrows, spears and guns, but their main weapon and symbol was the sword. Samurai were supposed to lead their lives according to the ethic code of Bushido ("the way of the warrior"). Strongly Confucian in nature, Bushido stressed concepts such as loyalty to one's master, self-discipline and respectful, ethical behavior. Many samurai were also drawn to the teachings and practices of Zen Buddhism—but that all came later.

Nara Period Art in Japan was ahead of the Art in Europe at the time. They were also ahead in Literature, Art and Politics. They had temples with 53 foot tall Buddhas in them. Literature was made up of Historical Documents, but they also wrote poetry. Some 4,000 poems were composed during this time in various styles. People of all walks of life were both the authors and subjects of these poems. It was often emotional.

WAKA was a form of Japanese Poetry. It had lines of 5, 7,5, 7 and 7. The First Three Lines of the WAKA made the HAIKU. Poetry was considered an activity like drinking or socializing. They would often divide up the syllables among people and link verses. Japanese asymmetry is buying 3 or 5 of something. The US likes things in 2, 4, 6 or 12. Japanese love odd numbers.

Also Japanese Gardens are not like English Gardens. The Japanese Gardens look more natural and are not done Geometric Shapes. They seek to blend romance and nature. Autumn is associated with dying. Cherry blossoms are associated with the fleeting nature of things. Spring and Fall both represent changes in Japan. The Tea Ceremony and Flower arranging are also traditions rooted in these ideas.

January 10, 1996 Heian Period and Culture

Heian Period is 794AD to 1185. It is divided in to two smaller periods 1) Siacho (764 to 822) and 2) Kukai (774-835). The Capital moved from Nara to Heian. Heian is the old word for Kyoto. Nara had become too crowded. They needed more room. Monasteries, Temples and Courts grew land wise and power wise during this time. Monks were interested in politics. One Monk involved with the Emperor's daughter reached the highest political level in the king-dom. He wanted to be Emperor. The Emperor was worried. They moved the Capital away from the meddling monks. Male members of the court began to distrust women and took their power away. Women had far more power in the Nara period than in the Heian Period.

Kyoto is surrounded by Mountains and is well protected. Kyoto is in a valley. The monasteries are in the mountains and not down in the valley with the Capital, which is by design. Saicho was an import monk who tried to protect Nara. He moved to Kyoto in order to protect that city as well. Eventually he was sent to China to study Buddhism in 804AD. The Japanese word for New Buddhism is Tendai on Mount Hiei. Hiei is an active temple and tourist destination today.

Tendai is a very popular school of Buddhism. The Emperor supported and even pushed for it. There is a connection to the Mahayana Tradition. Most important Sutra is Lotus. Buddha's Last Sermon is about how everyone has the potential to be Buddha. You have to be open and do charitable works, study texts and go into seclusion for 12 years.

The Emperor's second favorite monk was Kukai. He was sent to China too. He brought back a different form of Buddhism. He was known as a poet, inventor and explorer. He knew Sanskrit like most monks. Sanskrit is used to make endings of verbs and adjectives in Japanese language. Kukai and Saicho were competitors. Kukai had a pupil sent to him that was Saicho. Kukai kept Saicho, but refused to give him the knowledge he needed.

Kukai's Buddhism was Tantric Buddhism. It was Esoteric for the initiated. Sin Jon is correct or secret magic. There are the three mysteries of life—speech, body and mind. Tantric was only taught master to pupil. True words and postures of meditation are what is important. You have to be in the right frame of mind. It is a magical way of looking at Buddhism—a sort of cosmic Buddhism. Kukai's Monastery is in the Southern Mountains and are popular among the Aristocrats due to its exclusiveness.

Tendai had to develop his own esoteric brotherhood in order to compete with Kukai's. Part of Buddhism is the use of Mandalas, which are hanging scrolls used in meditation. Kukai used a flower tossed on another flower on a Cosmic Buddha for his Mandala. It signified thought carrying the message of Buddha.

Temples recruited peasants. Heian Period made it easier to become monks. Sects even had their own armies. There were small battles over religion through the mountains. Medera was burned several times in the battle and rebuilt.

There was corruption in the Nara Period, but even more so during the Heian Period. During the Medieval Period it increased even more. Even more Buddhist Sects popped up. In the Medieval Period Buddhism moved toward peasants. Shinto was still popular and used during spring and fall prayers. The Shrine of Esa was rebuilt.

Mappo was about the later days of the Buddhist Pureland Civilizations flourish for a bit, declined and disappeared. Pureland Buddhism gained traction. Buddha asked you to join and become enlightened. This Pureland Buddhism was more like Christianity in that belief in Amida Buddha was enough. You didn't have to study the texts or do any good deeds. You only have to think about it to be saved. Nemototsu.

People are supposed to look at pictures of Amida Buddha as they are dying. Three pictures are of Amida Buddha being saved like Jesus saving Christians. Buddhism even has a prayer necklace similar to a rosary. There are also pictures of a Phoenix welcoming people into the Pureland (Heaven) as well.

Buddha is heavy set with a mysterious expression on his face. Later, Buddha appears softer, friendlier and more approachable.

During the Heian Period Japan cut off relations with China. China was engaged in Civil Wars. The Japanese didn't feel a need to go and bring back more Civilization from China. They felt they no longer needed the Guidance of China.

The Japanese Imperial Family was isolated by their own choice. They didn't want to venture out. All the prestige positions were in Kyoto. The forgotten lower status of people often left. Some left and still had power, but not many. Usually a handful of representatives were sent out to deal with other Providences, but that was it.

Literature was unique during this period. Art, poetry and literature all flourished. This was the rise of the Clan Fujiwara. The can dominated the imperial marriage through marriage. Their daughters married into the imperial family and they wielded power through their grandchildren. They had one or more wives or letters wife #1 would be the most important and the children would be raised in her household. Fujiwara had lots of power.

Values include:

Miyabi: General Term that means Courtliness. It applied to the Upper Class mostly. It means elegance that is subtle and overt. It is not so casual.

Mono No Aware: It means a variety of things. It is a general sensitivity. It is a tinge of sadness or a soft sorrow. English word closest to it is Melancholy. It is finding beauty in that sadness. It is not extreme.

Okashi: It is something that is funny or amusing.

We know a lot of these aesthetics or values from novels and books written during this time in Japan.

The novel *Tale of Genji (1021AD)* was written during this period. This first novel was written by a woman. She was a lady of the court. Genji, the title character, is a man. He has many lovers. Genji is concerned about how well he spoke, carried himself and how well he wrote poetry. If your poetry wasn't written well then it meant your relationship probably wouldn't go well either.

Most of the literature during this time was short. *Tale of Genji* was the exception. The Japanese didn't develop novels very much. They understood plot and knew it wouldn't always go in a linear direction. Most of the novels out of Japan were episodic though. Modern Japanese novels are largely novelettes or novellas.

In 905 AD there was the *Waka Anthology* or *Kokinshu*. We have a sample of it in our textbook. See page 56. It is a refined and more suggestive than direct. There is no anguish or anger.

There were also private diaries. A lot of women wrote in diaries about their love life or about romance in general. The earliest diary known came from 935AD by Tosa. There was a boat trip taken. Poetry was interspersed among the diary entries. A man pretending to be a woman because women didn't write in Chinese wrote it.

The Gossamer Years was written in the late 900s. It was written by a Fujiwara son. It deals with a relationship—mostly centered on the husband. The husband and wife grew apart and then got back together.

Tale of Ese is a book with short episodes in it. These are probably things that really happened, although the focus is on Romance.

Running Bush was pillow talk. It was written by a woman—a lady in waiting. It was Okashi or funny.

Anyway, art became more secular during the Heian Period. An example was a hand painted scroll. There were stories and pictures on the scroll kind of like a comic book or graphic novel. Usually the scrolls have famous stories on them that everybody knew. They were easily read. The most famous scroll illustrations came from the *Tale of Genji.*

Entertainment for the Upper Classes included painting. Often times portrayals of people made their faces expressionless. They painted houses as if ceilings were gone. They gave bird's eye view of places. Moods of the paintings were often refined and subtle. Rooms were divided and slanted. They often expressed isolation. They use ribbons fluttering to represent turbulence. To appreciate Eastern Art, Westerners need to know about Miyabi or Elegance and Refinement.

The Public Buildings had a Chinese style to it. They had red tiled roofs. Homes in Japan often had a thatched roof and wooden floor. The pillar were unpainted. Homes were often built off the ground. There would be a garden next to the home. A stream with a pond would run underneath the house. That was a natural air conditioner.

January 16, 1996 Reviews
January 17, 1996 Quiz 1

January 18, 1996 Medieval Period History and Culture

The Medieval Period was from 1185 until 1600. The Providences become powerful. There was not enough power in Kyoto for their ambition. Families joined together and fought against each other for land and power. Two main families controlled Honshu. Minamoto. Taira was the Central Western Part.

There was instability that changed society. They were no longer sophisticated or refined. Homes and people both changed. There was lots of death and destruction. The Buddhist Sects during the Heian period couldn't survive.

Pureland Buddhism gained in Popularity. Nembutsu. There was controversy over rather you just said it once or if you had to say it many times. Shinron, a monk from Kyoto, was a man who settled the Nembutsu controversy. He said as long as your heart was sincere that was all that mattered. Shinron had a crisis and a vision. The vision told him to get married and stay religious. He ended up having 6 kids! He was the first Buddhist Monk to ever get married. He was exiled for it because the government thought he was a threat. His belief could be criminal! Two of Shinron's disciples fell in love with court women and they were killed. Shinron preached while he was in exile, he just didn't have his monk's robe. His nickname was "short haired and foolish." Monks were always bald, but he grew his hair out. Gu Toko. People called him hypocritical. He said he was aware of his self-centeredness and that nobody was perfect. He taught about wisdom and virtue. Humans make these values as they go along. He said you couldn't rely on yourself for enlightenment. You have to rely on Amida Buddha. We're not perfect, but Amida Buddha is.

Nichiren has its origins in Japan. Nichiren was a monk in Japan. He studied the Lotus Sutra and thought it was the most important. His chant was "Praise to the wonderful law of the Lotus Sutra." Spread the word! He was exiled and nearly assassinated. He had a death sentence, but escaped. Other Buddhist Sects thought their version of Buddhism was best. Nichiren hated other Buddhist Sects and had many enemies. Nichiren thought he was the new Buddha though. He was popular with some 6 million followers.

All realms of reality exist in a single moment. The past, present and future are all in your mind. You can reach a singularity through meditation. Meditation can also help you can physical wealth as well Nichiren stayed popular throughout the ages. Its popularity actually increased after WWII.

Zen Buddhism influenced the Warrior Culture more than any other. It had the patronage of the ruling class and the Shogun. The Masters of War were Zen. They were all about Zen Warriors were involved in trade and politics. Being Zen meant prestige. There were also Zen scholars who lived in Monasteries and Places of Learning.

January 22, 1996 Film The Japanese Tea Ceremony

The Tea Ceremony is kind of like a wine tasting. Everyone drinks tea, then drink saki and then do the community bathing thing. Green Tea is very popular in Japan. Black Tea is the other Tea they use. They prefer to use native ceramic cups—although they used to import their china from China. The making of the tea and serving of the tea is done in the same room in front of everyone. They use bamboo utensils to stir the tea. It is formalized and is supposed to be more spiritual stylistic.

A live ember or coal is put in a container with ash on a tray. There is water in bamboo. The container has a silk bag in it for strong tea. They open the container during the ceremony and serve the Tea in a bowl. The Tea House is called Imote Sinka. There are often 2 feet tall doorways that lead to the small room. There are racks for

Samurai Swords. The principles of the Tea Ceremony are implicity, Modesty and Harmony. There is also a sunken hearth in the middle of the floor. If the dry leaves are thick the tea will be strong. If the dry leaves are thin than the tea is weaker. The grind the leaves with a hand held grinder and create a powder from the leaves.

There is a changing room where people wait for the Host or Hostess. They go from the changing room to the Tea House. Tokubi is a stone basin. They rinse the tea to cleanse the sprits, etc. There are hot bowls at the middle entrance. They are guest bowls. The guests clean their hands and then go to the inner garden before being seated. The Hostess comes in gives a formal garden. The hostess uses a crane feather to dust the hearth and check the condition of ash.

Hostess brings water to the appropriate temperature and keep it at this temperature. Sometimes Ash will be mixed with the Tea during the summer. The Ash is stored in a wooden pail. October through November they have the Ash ready for sifting. Then they put kettle on the hearth and add incense to the hearth fire.

A meal is served after the arrangement of coals. The rocks are moved toward the bosom. They warm the rocks in front of Kimono to keep them warm Dinner Soup and three dishes are served. Soki and White Rice are served. The meal is kept light to barely fill you up. They serve wine a wooden tray.

The guests meat in the garden after they eat in a sort of intermission. The host prepares the room. She will sweep the room and open the skylight. They are making a change from Yang to Yin or from Dark to Light. The hostess will change her Kimono and strike the gong seven times—each time a different volume. It lets guests know that they are ready for them. The guests come back in and behave as if they are in the presence of a King or Holy Person. The guests sit down after the 7th Gong Ring.

The guests watch the host mix the Tea into paste. The Hostess makes sure that the guests see the utensils. The sound of the boiling water sounds like the wind through the pine trees. It is all about enjoying the quiet beauty and simple motions.

The guests sip from the same bowl of strong Tea. Dry sweet cakes are served as a weaker Tea is made. Bamboo is used to whisk the weak Tea. An assistant brings the weak Tea to the guests. The guests thank the host and bid farewell. The host leaves and then the guests leave. The host watches them leave silently. The Ceremony comes to an end.

There is no talking during the ceremony. It is all very low key and quiet. It is very meditative. Everyone who enters is automatically of the same social standing and humble. Each person will drink from a different side of the bowl that they share. Sometimes a scroll will be used in the ceremony and a poem will be read.

The Tea Ceremony is not usually something you pay to take part in. Though they will ask for donations or patronage to cover expenses. It is a social event. The Tea Ceremony is something more women than men take a class in. That is why there are most hostesses instead of hosts. The class on the Tea Ceremony teaches discipline, grace and concentration.

The Tea Ceremony is similar to Noh Theater and Landscaping. They all became popular and were developed in the Medieval Period.

January 23, 1996 Film The Principles and Practices of Zen

Wabi is austerity. Sabi is loneliness. Yugen is mystery or depth. Noh Theater. The Buddhist believes life is full of suffering. That is why they honor the old beat up utensils in the Tea Ceremony. The Samurai were the fighting class. They were not interested in refinement though. Zen Buddhism appealed to them.

Architecture of the medieval period included dry landscaping around houses. They had Zen Rock and Sand Gardens. The old Japanese Gardens included water in the form of a stream and a pond. In Zen, the dry austere landscape took over. The Zen had Ryoanji Temple where Monks and others were supposed to sit and meditate. The rocks were like islands in the pool of sand. The Japanese didn't design with geometry in mind.

Rush mats used Totomi. Shoji are thin rice paper doors. They are like paper and let light in. Mats and paper doors were often replaced. The Tearoom may also serve as a Living Room type place.

Noh Theater often featured religious themes like demon exorcism and reincarnation. The plays feature Buddhas, Kamis and Bodhisattvas. Once Noh Theater appealed only to upper classes. Sometimes homosexual relationships were portrayed. Shogunate was attracted to the Father/Son stories.

Yogen means mystery or the loss of mystery in a play. It is difficult to understand and is often very symbolic. Example is a plot about a ghost haunting a place. He stayed because of love. He is released from the world after the retelling of his story.

Kabuki and Noh Theater are usually made up of all male players or performers. However, Noh was mostly done in the Medieval Times while Kabuki came later.

In Europe the long sword was created to stab and chop. In Japan the Samurai or Katana are designed to slice and are very sharp. Using a Katana is an art form. A warrior would have a long sword as well as a short sword. They are basically a razor blade with a handle.

There were two types of Samurai. The Old Samurai were just out for the kill and were as quick as possible. They evolved in choreographed styles. They use short precise moves. They would study the moves for two years with the sword in the Sheath. A Samurai had respect for their swords and other weapons. Once they mastered swordplay they could show off. The fancy stuff that was done for show made it into Kurosawa's film *Rashoman*.

The Feudal Period was 268 years long from 1600-1868. It was equivalent to all of America's history—or nearly. The Samurai evolved during this this time. Their fighting was mean and they warriors were mostly concerned with keeping their lives. The time period was also known as the Tokugawa Time.

Bushido was the "way of the warrior." It was all about cultivating the mind and the character. These were top of the class students—the elite. Tokugawa united Japan, but Japan also cut themselves off from the rest of the world during this time.

Surprisingly, Christianity reached Japan around1542, before they closed their doors to the west. The Portuguese came with Jesuit Priests. The Jesuits had some 5,000 converts by 1630. Franciscan or Spanish Monks, Protestant Dutch and Protestant English visited Japan. During the European Age of Exploration, Explorers sailed to India and China—eventually making it all the way to Japan. The Chinese called the Europeans Southern Barbarians or "Nan-ban." They brought muskets, accurate maps, clothes, music, exotic animals, glasses, bread and tobacco to the East.

Christianity destabilized Japan with competing groups trying to convert. They mostly arrived in Keshu—the Southern Island. Groups accused each other of various things and bad mouthed each other frequently. Christianity was banned from Japan in 1617. By 1638 it was virtually erased from Japan. Some 5,000 to 6,000 Japanese Christians were killed. Japan closed its doors and would not allow

Japanese citizens to even return home. Big ships were forbidden. Only small fishing ships were allowed to be used or owned by Japanese Citizens.

Endo Snusak wrote *"Silence."* He was a Christian. He is the author of 3% of all Japanese-Christian literature. Silence was about a Portuguese Priest who went to Japan and abandoned his faith. Why did he abandon his faith? Men followed him and tried to find him, but he was oppressed—silenced by the Japanese Government.

Centralized Feudalism consisted of The Shogun at the top followed by Saimyo, Vasseles and then the Peasants. One of the three Important Military Leaders of the Time were Oda Nodnaga, Hidegoshi, Tokugawa and Calletral. Nodnaga was assassinated by one of the Generals. Hidegoshi was a ruthless General from a poor family. He divided the land into Fiefs and gave the land to the Patrons. He took arms or weapons from his peasants. He had lots of power to tell what to do. He could even tell his followers to commit suicide. When Hidegoshi died, there was a power struggle and bloody warfare. Tokugawa took over in the early 1600s and made Tokyo the Capital. He had 245 to 295 Daimyos underneath him.

Finally, in 1868, Japan opened itself up to the world and to the west. They wanted to learn the ways of modern men. Why? 1) To Increase Secular and Nonreligious Buddhism among intellectuals 2) To spread Confucianism, which was taught by the Zen Monks and 3) Justification for Feudal Ruling of Country.

January 24, 1996 Zen Movie

Intensive Meditation takes place during the 12 months of the year. The year goes from January 15th until December 15th. The goal was to see a star during their meditation as Buddha did under the Bodhi tree. Monks will sit for 7 days like it is a single day. Discipline was important. The monks would pledge to devote themselves only to meditation. A Zen Priest must enter a monastery to get training to be a priest. You must ask permission to enter at the Entrance of any Monastery. You can stay if permission is given. Sometimes they say no to test your dedication. Meditation can lead to Satori or Enlightenment. It is obtained by the seeker through strength and determination.

After 3 Days of Refusal, our seeker is finally admitted. He will undertake the Master/Pupil relationship with a Monk. The Master

Monk is treated like a Buddha. The Disciple will not leave the Monastery until he reaches Enlightenment. Zen is only relative to moment you seek Enlightenment. Totomi mat is the only possession a Monk will be allowed to have. Rensi is a special center and Shogengi is one of them. Like a grove of trees, students will strive further when isolated from society.

A Day In The Life: There is a 3am wake up call. He has not slept for 7 days. He gets refreshed and has a breakfast of Rice from a large cauldron around 5am. Disciples have to do the heavy labor of cooking for the Monastery. Before each meal they chant. It is kind of like saying Grace. They put aside three pieces of rice for the Hungry Spirits. When they eat they observe the Hall of Silence. There is no talking whatsoever. After the meal, they drink tea and clean their dishes. They mediate after breakfast and search themselves for the truth. They sit in Zazen.

The idea is to unify the body and the mind through breathing. It is important to take long, deep breath. The body should be not too hot or too cold—comfortable. Rambling thoughts are pushed away. The quietening of the mind is important. Monks may also learn to meditate while walking or doing other every day activities.

To get rid of sleepiness, the monks eat a mid-day meal around 10:30am. No animal products are consumed. EVER. They meet with the Zen Master 4 times a day from 4 to 9pm. The master gives him a problem. The Disciple must give an answer. If he comes up with the wrong answer, the master must correct him. Two minds meet in intense conformation here. The bell will be rung if the answer given is correct.

It is all about finding the Buddha inside. It is important to bring the outside Buddha into inside Buddha awareness. The mind should be expanded and able to think new thoughts. The use Koans Like what is the sound of one hand clapping?

Gekitgutzo uses the warning stick. He uses it to rouse the spirit. He uses it to relax stiffened muscles and keep his disciples awake during meditation. Later, they drink Rice Wine, which is served warm. They offer service to the Buddha—who is the symbol of enlightenment. Those who also become enlightened are called Bodhisattva. It is a difficult path that requires much discipline.

It is 12 midnight before the disciples are able to take a brief rest. Nothing is wasted here: Not loyalty, quietness or strength.

Film Ends.

Brief word from Guest Speaker: Natsuko Konishi has a small child who is a Summer Child. Her husband transferred to Mansfield, Ohio a year ago. She talked about going to a Buddhist Temple. The temple is mostly a Shrine to the New Year and for Funerals. Although Families tend to go to the same Temple for generations, younger people in Japan have stopped going. She does believe in the Pure Land version of Buddhism. Konishi studied English in Junior High. The English Spoke in her class is different from the English spoken here in Ohio. It is the difference between *How are you? And How are you doing?* She says that Americans have a tendency to exaggerate. The Japanese are more modest.

January 25, 1996 Meiji Restoration and Reform

The Tokugawa Period was from 1600 until 1860. The Meiji Period was from 1868 to 1912. There were peasants. Rice growers were fed up with paying taxes. The Samurai classes not like the merchants and couldn't raise taxes. The Samurai were taking money from the peasants for themselves. The pecking order or hierarchy: Samurai, Peasants and Merchants. Jobs that centered on animal slaughter was considered "polluted." Anything centering on death was "polluted."

Bushido translates to "way of the warrior." Bushido meant a warrior was supposed to be moral and upstanding. Loyalty to the Samurai came first even above loyalty to one's family.

The Story of the 47 Ronin is famous. A Ronin is a Master-less Samurai. 47 Samurai vowed revenge on a Lord who was wounded by a stranger ignorant to their ways. All 47 committed suicide. After they murdered the Lord, they committed suicide by disemboweling themselves. The Japanese love stories of suicide—often romanticize it. It is a noble end to them.

The Samurai participated and developed arts. They participated in the writing of Haiku, flower arranging and theater.

Edo is the cultural and business center of Tokyo. It became the center of the Military Dictatorship. The Samurai did not approve the idea of the floating worlds. If you had money you could go to the floating world.

Ukiyo-e is a genre of Japanese Art, which flourished from the 17th through 19th centuries. Its artists produced woodblock prints and paintings of such subjects as female beauties; kabuki actors and sumo wrestlers; scenes from history and folk tales; travel scenes and landscapes; flora and **fauna**; and **erotica**. The term *ukiyo-e* translates as *"pictures of the floating world."* It was a productive time. Spas, Baths, Theaters and Tea Houses thrived in addition to wood block paintings.

Famous Artists in Japan include Hokusai who did 36 views of Mt. Fuji. Hiroshige did 36 Stations on the Tokaido. The Tokaido Highway is a popular subject matter. There are wondering entertainers, priests and Daimyos. Literature from the Floating World was like Harlequin Romances. It was racy and there were loose morals.

Textiles included the Silk Industry. Poor people used cotton Kimonos. The rich were able to afford silk Kimonos. Silk was sometimes used in Kabuki Theater. The theater was for everybody and portrayed everyday people. It was stylized. Male actors played both male and female rolls though. Women used to play themselves until it caused chaos. Their sexuality was distracting. So young boys would play women. It was considered a necessary evil.

The Meiji Period from 1868 until 1912 occurred at the end of the Tokugawa Period. Japan signed a treaty for Friendship—well Commercial Friendship. 1) Americans were given the right to given to be tried for a crime. This is a disadvantage for Japan. 2) Americans were allowed to carry arms in Japan even though the Japanese were not. A boy was flogged for having a weapon in 1992 or 1994. 3) Most favored the Nation Clause. It prevented one Western Nation from having advantages over the other Western nations. 4) Goods were only given a 5% tax if both parties agree. It was an unequal treaty.

There were lots of imports into Japan. Japan did export some silk. There was opposition to the treaty. A lot of opposition from Daimyos who were not friendly with Tokugawa. He was once friendly with missionaries. Rebellion occurred. Satsuma and Choshu were leaders of the families who rebelled. Loyalists to Kyoto showed support for the Emperor.

The 1868 Rebellion was a relatively bloodless revolution. The two families walked into Kyoto and took over. They put a boy on throne. The boy's name was Meiji. They use the calendar from when he was Emperor. This Emperor was revered. He got rid of the barbarians. There was nostalgic feelings of going back to Japan's glory days. They dismantled the feudal system. Daimyos remained as Governors of their domains or prefectures.

Commoners were allowed to have last names. The title of Outcast banned. Now peasants had the freedom to grow whatever crop they want. Christianity is legalized in 1868. The Samurai were no longer able to wear swords out of hereditary bureaucracy. The soldiers were now military based.

Some BIG CHANGES took place. There was a big rebellion in 1877. The Samurai were unhappy when they did away with the army. It was not a bloody rebellion. Samurai wanted a divine Emperor to regain old glory.

They eventually realized they needed to look to the West for inspiration. Then there was a big enthusiasm to Modernize. They put up telegraph lines and street lights. They built post offices Most importantly, they built up their military with munitions and artillery.

They adapted to Western Styles as well. The men cut their hair short and grew out facial hair. They started eating beef. They built brick houses and outlawed co-ed public bathing. They borrowed police and military uniforms from the West as well. Men were the first to wear everyday Western clothing. Then women were allowed to eventually.

Japan sent their own to the US to learn more about the West. There was a book about a young Japanese Girl who went to the West to Study in the US for 10 years. The Government needed to sponsor Westernization. Why did they send Mothers and Children? All the young men in Japan had government jobs. The Japanese Women had trouble fitting into the US. Some found a place teaching. Deer Cry Mansion was built by the Japanese Government. It had meeting rooms, a ball room and, of course, hotel rooms. Another young Japanese woman set up a school for women. Some women worked as professors at Universities.

Christian Missionaries returned to Japan. Japan opened an agricultural college in Hokkaido. The professors were Western and Christian. Only about 4% of the Japanese are Christian. Some of the Japanese believed the West could do no wrong, which was a naive way of looking at things. When they re-opened up to the West, they were a bit pickier.

Japanese returned to teaching Confucianism, which included teaching honor and loyalty. Japan believed they were superior. Their Emperor was a deity. The average person was not involved in politics. They did create a Parliament and a Constitution, but they were of limited power. Although the US was influential, so was Germany. The House of Peers was appointed and the House of Representatives was elected. The Bureaucracy centered on Tokyo University. The Houses pick the Prime Minister. The Military Assassinated 3 of the Prime Ministers. It was the Military who put people in power or took them out of power. The system was very flawed.

Japan went to war against China 1894 until 1895. Japan won and annexed Taiwan and Manchuria. They also had sway or influence in Korea. Britain took back their treaties after that. The war proved to the West that Japan wasn't going to be pushed around.

The Novel developed in Europe and American in the 1800s. British, Russian and American novels were translated into Japanese so that they had access to Western Literature. The Novel wasn't considered as important as history or poetry. Poetry was written in China and Japan by men in the Chinese language. Novels written in Japan were stereotypical. No real character development. Writers described emotions and plots in standard Tokyo dialect. Print was cheap then so books, magazines and newspapers were readily available in the late 1800s and early 1900s.

There was a famous writer who wrote *Natsume Soseki,* This was a book about the Japanese problems modernizing. People in Japan were lonely and isolated.

In the late 1890s and early 1900s the Meiji Miracle happened. Not many people opposed the war on China. The Japanese were extremely proud. In 1896 Russia, Germany and France forced Japan to give Manchuria back. The triple intervention upset Japan—particularly Russia's involvement. Japan became more Nationalistic. There were some pacifists who were socialists in Japan, but Japan banned Socialism.

In 1904 and 1905 Japan went to war with Russia. They got Manchuria back and all of Korea. It was annexed in 1910. They had use of Russian railroads. It was a source of pride. Japan had a lot of little colonies here and there. The Japanese Government ran propaganda and conscripted or drafted many soldiers for their army. The Japanese were optimistic, but then WWI came along.

Japan didn't really participate in the European Warfare. It wasn't until the Treaty of Versailles that they were included. Some of the German-Asian South Pacific Islands were given to the Allies.

Japan had a recession after WWI. There was a food shortage, absentee landlords and high rents. They had a very uneven Industrial Revolution. It had a duel structure economy. Some people benefited nicely from comfy factory jobs. Some people had no access to technology. They worked making crafts or agriculture.

Zalbotsky was like the Monopolies in the US. Longloment had lots of companies underneath them. Power was in the hands of a few and they influenced the government. They gave money to political parties. They co-operated with the West to get access to new raw materials. The Governments juggled powerful groups. Zaibots wanted Peace in the West, but still built up Military. They were a Pro-Emperor group.

The culture of the 1920s was peaceful. The Japanese opened up communication and education. Things were peaceful. They dabbled in publishing, entertainment business, sports, radio and films. Then in the late 1920s the situation changed. International trade started to decline. The stock market crashed. The population swelled to 55 Million in Japan, which was too much. They were overpopulated. To make matters worse the US stopped letting Japanese and Chinese immigrants into the US. The famine hit and they couldn't adjust like they did before. No nation could survive by consuming more than they could produce.

This made the Japanese felt threatened. They also feared that Russia and China were going to gang up on them. Capitalism was beginning to lose its luster. Japan took it as a sign that it was time to expand their empire.

The Japanese Army finally took action in 1931. The railroad tracks were bombed in Manchuria. The Japanese invaded Manchuria and blamed China. China had set up a puppet state and Japan hadn't stopped them. The peasants were all gun-ho for expansion. Leaders were assassinated and parliament disintegrated. It was a slow process of intimidating people until they had no power. The army and navy moved in after the Oligarchy died off. The New Oligarchy was the Military. The Ultra-nationalists were fascists. It was not like in Italy or Germany though. There was no singular charismatic leader or major support. It was simply that the Japanese Military took the power.

The Japanese stopped teaching English in School. Today there are people in their 60s who have trouble with English. They don't have the education. Buddhism and Christianity fell out of favor. They had a State Shintoism. There was a Network of Shinto Shrines. They taught their ideology and myths through Shinto. Patriotism was mixed with mysticism and heredity.

In the early 1930s Japan increased their exports some. The League of Nations criticized Japan and so Japan pulled out of it in 1933. In 1938 there was a new order in East Asia. Japan decided to take over some Chinese Capitals, but they never conquered China completely. In 1940 Great Asia wanted to take over Australia, New Zealand and the South Pacific Islands. They acted quickly and made a PAC with Axis Powers. This led to Anti-Japanese sentiment in the US. The US put an expert Embargo on Japan. The US created Concentration Camps.

Major decisions were made at liaison conferences. Emperors and Ministers were at the Liaison Conference. The Ministers were at the table and the Emperor was behind a screen. If the Emperor approved of the decision he would bang a golden seal gong. The Emperor wasn't supposed to talk. He couldn't ask questions or give opinions. There was no honest exchange and no real communication.

The decision was made to form an alliance with the Nazis in 1940. There was no real plan—just confusion and doubt. The army and navy worked separately. The US had more resources than Germany and Japanese people in the US were afraid of being penalized or killed for speaking out against the war. Japan saw America as way get the resources they needed—the raw material needed to survive. That is what lead to them directly attacking America. They viewed is as a strategic strike, but they underestimated the response by the USA.

Japan was surprised that that the US fought back as quickly and strongly as they possibly could. The Pacific Theater of the War began. 2,400 people died during the Pacific Theater. Japan lost some 25,000 people and the US lost over 5,000 on various islands across the ocean. Americans increased their firepower. It was bloody fighting as Japanese never surrendered. Kwajalein saw Japan lose 8,500 and the Americans lost 300. Leyte saw 300 dead. Iwa Jima saw Japan lose 1800 and the US lost 5,000.

January 30, 1996 Film Hiroshima: The Legacy

The tide of the battle changed at the Battle of Midway. It was June of 1942. They were able to decode the Japanese messages. Americans gained control of the situation. In 1942 the Emperor of Japan was told he could not win. It wasn't until 1943 that the Military was told they couldn't win, but still no action was taken.

In November of 1944 Guam happened. American bombed Japanese Cities. 10,000 people were killed in this first bombing. The air raids continued 600,000 Japanese died. 9 Million People were homeless. They didn't want to surrender, as evident by Kamikaze pilots. Civilians used bamboo spears and arrows. The Allies continued putting pressure on them.

Churchill estimated some 1 million casualties and Truman only estimated ½ a million. Meanwhile, Japan lost more than 4 million! Truman signed the order to use the Atomic Bomb. There was no conversation or debate about it. No one questioned the morality of using such a terrible weapon of mass destruction. It wasn't clear exactly what would happen when they denoted it over a city filled with people.

August 6, 1945 the Enola Gay dropped the Atomic Bomb on Hiroshima. Then on August 9, 1945 we dropped another Atom Bomb on Nagasaki. 80,000 people were killed immediately. They surrendered unconditionally. Some 4 Million Japanese lost their life in WWII. In comparison there were 6 Million Jews killed in the Holocaust.

There is a museum in Hiroshima dedicated to Peace. There are 6,000 relics. At 8:15am that daytime stopped. The working day began at 8am in the city. 400,000 people lived in Hiroshima. It was the 3rd Largest City in Japan. It was completely destroyed. Utter desolation. The Bomb detonated 800 feet above the city Hospital. It blew outward and then sucked back inward.

The ensuing fireball was hot enough to melt iron! Walls were knocked out of place. Glass was shattered. Skin was burned and left hanging off people's bodies. The intense flash left shadows behind on walls of human figures and other objects. Clothes and trees burst into fire. People were burned alive. Those who survived took 4 months or more to heal. They had keloids and bumps all over. They had black nails with veins in them.

Not a blade of grass grew in Nagasaki or Hiroshima for 75 years! People volunteered to come and knock down the ruined buildings. Students helped clear away debris. The only things left intact were first aid kits and tin lunch boxes. The food inside the lunch box was all carbonized.

Black rain fell in the area for years. Anyone who had the black radioactive rain fall on them experienced a great deal of pain. The rain caused injury and death to many that survived the blast. The radiation caused horrible painful deaths to thousands in the fallout area. They suffered with blotches, bleeding, puss and extreme pain before death. Their gums bled, their teeth fell out and they had open sores covering their body. Cancer consumed many. Some had hair loss for 2 to 8 weeks before dying of Thyroid Cancer.

It was said that the Atomic Bomb was used in order to shorten the war and save thousands of lives. But did it do that? It seems, in retrospective, as if the war against Japan was already won and that some American lives might have been saved, but at what cost? Could the war have ended another way and still been a victory? Signs point to yes.

A land invasion and regular bombs would have done the job. American had spent a ton of money developing The Atomic Bomb with the Manhattan Project. Congress was demanding an investigation into where all the money went and if it was worth it. People who had spent so much money on the nuclear weapon wanted to see results. Dropping the bomb might have motivated by a fear of Russia.

In any case, Japan surrendered on August 14, 1945. Most of the important Military Leaders committed suicide. Others died of disease, torture or mere exhaustion because they were slave labor in Prison Camps. War Crimes had been committed by Japan and the Japanese had a difficult time apologizing. Local War Commissions sentenced a lot of their own to prison for these War Crimes.

Oscar Schindler helped Jews in Europe. One Japanese man did something similar. Sugihara got the Jews Visas from Japan so they could travel on the Burmese Railroad. The authorities told him no, but him and his wife issued the Visas anyway. Once the Japanese government figured out what he had done, they were embarrassed. Germany didn't like it much either. The Japanese Consulate Closed and Sugihara was made to leave. The Soviets captured him and sent him back to Japan. Lithuania gave him citizenship. He was a light bulb sales man later in life. He apologized to his widow for the "misunderstanding." He died in 1982.

January 31, 1996 Post War Japan: Occupation and Reform

Things were tough for Japan after WWII. 30% of population was homeless. All the major cities were bombed. Food was scarce and industry was all but destroyed. Inflation was High and things were Chaotic. People were confused. The Japanese were scared of Americans, but Americans tried to help them reform and recover.

Luckily, the Japanese were resilient. They turned their back on the Military that betrayed them and fell back on their High Education standards. The Pre-War Constitution allowed them to go back to a familiar democracy. Two major figures in this history include General Douglas MacArthur and Premier Yoshida.

So what were the Four Elements of Reform? The Military was stripped. The war industry in Japan was abolished. School Boards were decentralized. Finally, they worked to restore the Economy. The land that Japan had acquired was taken away. Some 6 1/2 Million Japanese were living on repossessed land. Okinawa was under American Occupation/Leadership.

They adopted some amendments to their constitution. They put in a system of checks and balances. They created a Bill of Rights. Included in this Bill of Rights was Women's Right To Vote in Japan. Essentially, anyone over the age of 20 could vote. Both Houses—the Upper House and House of Councilors—were elected. They had an independent judicial system and a supreme court. The Governors were elected and no longer appointed. The Police System was de-centralized. They added a clause called Article 9. It stated that Japan couldn't declare war except in Self-Defense. Most Japanese are okay with that.

They had Compulsory Education up to 9th Grade. In Japan they go 6 years for Elementary School, 3 Year for Junior High and 3 Year for High School. Then there is 4 Years of College. Their Textbooks were totally revised.

Some reforms didn't last after the war and occupation. Some things became Re-Centralized. Police and Education moved back toward Centralization. Some Absentee Farmers had to sell farms at Pre-War prices.

Reforming was more important than rebuilding at first. The Cold War was developing and the US needed Japan to be an Ally. In 1950 there was the Korean War. America wanted Japan to help them produce weapons or war supplies at least. The Occupation of Japan ended in 1951 with the San Francisco Peace Treaty. Russia wouldn't sign it though. In 1956 Japan was admitted to the UN. In the mid-1950s the economy kept going up 10% each year. in the 1960 Security Treaty renewed. There were protests in Japan. Some students protested nuclear power plants and nuclear weapons. There was definitely an anti-nuclear sentiment in Japan. They didn't want to be pulled into a war with the US. The Treaty was ratified and no new Nuclear Weapons were allowed without approval. Eisenhower canceled his visit to Japan.

At the End of the Post-War period Japan sponsored the 1964 Olympics. In the late 1960s there was student unrest and student protests over Vietnam. Japan didn't want to get pulled into Vietnam. In the 1970s Japan had a huge trade surplus. They invested abroad. In the 1980s if something was made in Japan, it meant it was quality.

People spent the 80s and early 90s trying to learn from Japan. They wanted to emulate their successful business models. They wanted to duplicate their Higher Education Program results. Good Business and Low Crime made Japan very appealing to the US and others.

In the 1980s Japanese films, foods, books, karaoke, karate and designers were all imported to the USA. Land values were high in the 80s, but collapsed a bit in the early 90s. The 90s have been a doldrums of economy in Japan and elsewhere. The Yen is overvalued. Japanese Imports are now more expensive.

February 1, 1996 Guest Speaker

We watched a home video of a wedding. It was an arranged marriage. It evolved from a blind date agreement. This is not the law in Japan, but it does happen frequently. They dated for only a short time and then got engaged. It took 4 months total from the time they met until they married.

The Ceremonial Kimono arrives a week before the wedding. She is wearing a Kimono Obi Belt. It has a stiff piece of cardboard in it. The Kimono dips in back. The back of the neck is thought to be very attractive in Japan. As in America, the bride had an engagement ring and a wedding band. The Bride is also wearing a traditional wig that is long with folds in it. It takes 4 hours total for her to get ready.

Oscashci is the colored jacket. It changes when she changes over to the house of her husband. This time she is wearing a white belt and the groom is wearing a white jacket. His Kimono has his family crest on it.

Her father runs the Shinto Shrine where they married. He is the 16th Generation to run that particular Shinto Shrine. There is a shelf in the temple with Shinto and Buddhist stuff. The Ceremony is just 30 minutes long. Only family attends the ceremony. The husband and wife go between bamboo containers with water. It symbolizes how she will go from her house to her husband's house once she is married. The two houses will combine.

After the Ceremony the Bride will change and they will go to the Reception. The Reception is 3 hours long. They will drink Sake three times and listen to Guga music. They will recite their vows in front of friends. The families will introduce themselves. There are a ton of speeches. The microphone is passed around the room and people will talk or sing. Some give comical speeches. There are Geisha dancers that perform. No dancing by the guests though. A Koto is played. It is an instrument like a harpsichord, but huge.

The Divorce Rate in Japan is really low.

February 5, 1996 Review
February 6, 1996 Quiz 2

February 7, 1996 Structure of Japanese Society

Groups are very important in Japan, where as Americans value Individuality. Americans do see groups playing a role in society with family, clubs, sports and other things. In Japan Family is front and center of society. It is everything. There are very few single parents. Mother, Father and Children are considered the nuclear family and are fundamental to Japanese Society. Work defines the Japanese much more than it does Americans. Japanese Companies stress loyalty and treat their employees like family. Team players are valued at Japanese Companies.

Alma Maters are important in Japan. High School and College inspire a great deal of loyalty. Many students have a strong connection to their places of education for 10 to 20 years after they graduate. Students rarely transfer from school to school. Most students also join a club or two. In college students get a chance to meet a possible spouse and network for future jobs. Alumni and other clubs help them get jobs after they graduate. Employers feel employees who join groups are good at working as a team and have good leadership skills.

Some Students join Religious Groups. They might join a Christian Group, but Shinto and New Buddhism are more popular. The groups provide support for the students and help them get jobs as well.

They don't have a lot of problem with violence. There are the Yakuza, which is like the Mafia. They deal with gambling, prostitution and guns. There aren't really any teen gangs. Juvenile Delinquents are few and far in between. The court goes easy on them. Most of the time their parents, who are deeply ashamed of their kid's behavior, discipline them. Some students suffer from extreme anxiety or school sickness. There is some unhappiness with the lack of flexibility in Japanese Society.

Drugs are not really a problem in Japan. Not many drugs are smuggled in and very little makes it to the High Schools. Teen Pregnancy is also not an issue. Birth Control is readily available. Abortion is also available, but the father of the baby needs to give his permission. Having a child out of wedlock is a big no-no in Japan. It is expected that students will graduate, go to college, get a job and then get married.

Women do have a fair amount of freedom. They can vote and go to college. They are encouraged to work and support themselves--at least until they get married. Kids don't watch a lot of TV. Parents are a huge influence on their children, more so than their peers. Children are dependent on their parents until age 18. Kids don't mind that much.

Japanese mothers let their children sleep with them in the same bed until they are a year old or so. Mothers keep their kids closer in

Japan than American mothers.

The Idea of Wa or Harmony in Japan is important. Consensus is important. You can't flat out tell people no, so you have to be polite about it. Maybe say, "Yes, but...." It is good to soften it. Japanese are careful not to insult anyone. Often they will use a go-betweens like a lawyer. However, the Japanese try to solve problems without going to court. The go-betweens do it as a favor mostly. They get nice gifts or whatever in return. Not an obligation though.

Japanese Ethics are more flexible in some ways. It is not black and white, as things tend to be in the USA. The Japanese see a balance in things--Yin and Yang. Everything is connected. They are not in conflict and they complement each other. Japanese see Americans as self-righteous, outspoken and overly critical. The US argues over abortion and the death penalty. Japan sees the USA as weak and lacking in principle. The Japanese rely on rules and codes of conduct. The have ethics. Punctuality is very important, as is courtesy.

Japan is changing though. Younger people show more affection in public and are more open to divorce. They embrace Western ways more so than the older generations.

February 8, 1996 Business Practice and Studies

Moto is the study of Japanese in American for business. Decision Making in Japanese Companies: joint ventures throughout the world especially US, need to understand Japanese national culture, WA is peace and harmony, amae is an indulgent love (spiritual and physical harmony) amae results in shinyo which refers to the mutual confidence, faith and honor required for successful business relationships, emphasis is on cooperation, participative management, consensus problem solving and decision making based on patient long term perspective, open expression of conflict is discouraged. It is very important to avoid embarrassment or shame, to lose face as a result of not fulfilling one's obligations. Culture of collectivism and shared responsibility that underlies the Japanese ringi system of decision making: group consensus, unlike Americans top-down individualistic perspective, very time consuming, slow progress is problematic when they are time sensitive, lots of time in the earlier phases of the process and consider 'big picture' rather than rushing into things like Americans, system designed to manage continuity and avoid uncertainty which is considered a threat to group cohesiveness.

Summary of key points 1: ability to negotiate, 2. The progression of the negotiation process and the prerequisite of building trusting relationships 3. Understanding different values perspectives and agendas importance of relationship building in different countries= imperial to understanding different perspectives, values and agendas of other parties and the use of problem solving approach. And to be able to negotiate various styles and tactics in exchanging task-related information- ringi system, top-down, verbal, nonverbal everyone likes to work as a team. You don't just go straight into business, relationship building is required therefore before a business transaction is made you may go out to eat, have a drink or some fun so that an underlying trust building foundation is developed. Risk tolerance in America is more likely because they are really rushed in their decision making process and therefore not everyone is consulted, and not enough time is dedicated into the 'big picture' of the decision.

For the Japanese there process is very long and time consuming and therefore in a very fast paced globalized business world their traditional system may be outlived the rush of when the decision needs to be made subjective influences the Japanese decision making process because they want to have a trust foundation and relationship with the people they are doing business with rather then thinking objectively and have no idea if the person you did business with is a legitimate trading partner America those who are at the bottom feel like robots following day to day tasks and there influence usually can't and wont make a difference and is not always appreciated. Japanese feel more involved and therefore makes them more enthusiastic about their work environment and partners for they are able to voice them opinion and in such a manner that they are able to without being embarrassed or ridiculed by their partner

Crowell's harsh handling of the dolls by looking away another form of Japanese business which involves less facial gazing. Why did Crowell's remarks about Allmack threaten a loss of face from Moto's perspective? In the Japanese culture your way of forming respect is through building relationships and trust. Crowell wanted to impress Moto by boasting, showing off and acting pretentious, which are just embarrassing in the Japanese mind. The topic of conversation was supposed to be about Allmack and Crowell made it revolve around himself, which simply was not of appeal to Moto. Therefore, their different ways of gaining status, the Japanese through relationships and Crowell through material achievements threatened loss of face for Moto. When Crowell lays out his business card Moto was trying to remain in good etiquette despite the arrogant and humiliating circumstance he was faced with. Moto, like a proper Japanese businessman kept things formal by keeping a stern face and not showing any emotions. This is an example of how the American's way of efficiency interferes with the Japanese process of business negotiation. Crowell wanted to send out the message that we was successful, show status and objectively, get straight down to doing business. On the other hand, Moto was expecting a time-consuming business process that involved mutually trusting relationship building, the very cornerstone of Asian business. This situation further symbolizes cooperation and respect vs. arrogance and superiority vs. urgency. This situation also had implications for it is apparent that they both do business at very different extremes and Crowell's boasting and impatience is not a positive way to collaborate in business with Moto. A loss of face is an important topic in shame cultures like japan. In their culture the "face" is related to the social recognition. Every Person has his face and it is built up with how other persons think of you and it can be withdrawn with losing your respect and being disregarded. Respect is an important part in this evaluation and with respecting someone else and regarding him you also gain recognition. So, the sudden decline of one's own prestige is called a loss of face. In our situation the loss of face is threatened by the different ways of gaining status in Japan and America. For the Japanese you gain status in business affairs through relationships and the Americans are more concerned about material achievements. Moto was expecting a process of getting to know each other and therefore building up trust and respect for each other. He tried to build up a relationship with handing out the cards and remarking each other's position and also bringing a present. Crowell rejected these efforts by just putting the card away and then immediately get to talk about Allmack. He boasted about how good they are and what Allmack already achieved. This was already an act of disrespecting Moto in the way of thinking that Moto was not already well informed about Allmack's record. Showing off and acting pretentious is also embarrassing in Japanese mindset. With that Crowell showed falling respect by his

February 13, 1996 Government and Politics

Change to Democracy came after Feudal Age. Japan was transformed completely in 100 years. There were no religious, ethnic or language barriers. Places like South Africa and Haiti had problems making the transition. Japan still has a central ruler--an emperor. The Emperor's power was shifted, but the centralization needed for bureaucracy was already in place.

The Japanese have strong Ethical beliefs. Confucianism influence the Government quite a bit. The Government did not bend to corruption and transcended into democracy with ease. They valued tradition, honesty and had high standards. Education was deeply valued and most people understood Confucianism. Although Shinto was generally accepted, it was not made the State Religion. And there were no civil wars or fractions fighting amongst themselves.

After the Military took over and lost WWII, a Prime Minister was put in place. The Minister can pick his cabinet and they will stay a year. They had a parliament like England, but also took inspiration from the American Constitution. The Upper House needs a 2/3rd vote majority to make amendments to their constitution. The Congress has committees and writes up Legislation. In Japan, Legislature is drafted by the Bureaucracy and then it gets voted on with a pass or non-pass. Japan also has a national court similar to the US Supreme Court. Although Japan doesn't have national, state, county and city court like the US. It is a much smaller area.

There are public prosecutors. They get a 99% confession rate. There is no plea bargaining. Rehabilitation is a huge part of their system. They consider what the family thinks and if the criminal shows any remorse. Judges are appointed by the Senate for life. The Supreme Court in Japan doesn't want to rule on abstract issues. They don't wish to have the role of shaping society.

Article 9: Clause that the Japanese cannot develop a Military Presence in order to attack. They can only raise a Military force in order to defend themselves from an attack by someone else. But this article has been side stepped a bit by the use of Peacekeeping Operational Forces. The Japanese allow their presence and contribute materials and people for the UN's use. They send Nurses, Doctors, Drivers and others to help with UN Peacekeeping Missions.

The Supreme Court in Japan did rule on Environmental issues. The Polluter must pay for the damages, but not exactly a crime. In the 1950s there was Mercury Poisoning in Minamata. A company dumped some 80 tons of Mercury. Many people suffered from Mercury Poisoning. They lost control of their arms and legs as well as their mental faculties. The victims took the company to court. The company denied the possibilities. Although the case was brought to court in the 1960s, the company didn't have to pay damages until the 1970s.

The Local Government is a bit different Taxes come from the main or central government. Local taxes are the law and most local government has office in Tokyo. State offices are set up in Tokyo as well. They get money to influence their states.

The Legislation of the central government suggests or models laws. They follow examples. The State Government gets money from the Central Government and isn't as independent as the Local Governments.

They have political parties as well. The Liberal Democratic Party was in power until 1993. The Collation Government is now in power. There is no single party in party. New Parties are LDP and DSP. New Parties came in since 1993 and the power structure changed.

There are not too many lawyers in Japan. They are few and far in between. US Lawyers often come over to Japan with the large corporations they work for. There aren't many law schools in Japan and those that do exist are very difficult to get into. Law Schools are state one. It is difficult to get work with international companies.

The Police are respected, but don't have a high prestige position. The Police force is made up of mostly men. There are very few women in the Police Force. Tokyo calls the Police Box the Koban. Policemen are close to everybody in the neighborhood or at least they are familiar with everyone who lives there. Koban or the idea of the Police Box is important to keeping crime low. They go door to door and give out surveys at least 2 times a year. They keep records who live where. They keep driver's licenses numbers and cars registered at what house or apartment. Neighborhood Watches are huge in Japan. The Police are also very visible on foot or bicycle

In Japan if you kill someone, you go to jail. Once the criminal gets out of prison, his or her family will disown them. There is no subculture that makes it "cool" to do crime. There are not a lot of pawn shops either. Police have authority and leeway to prosecute. They can arrest people without a warrant. They can be detained for 23 days with no access to a lawyer. They have 1,000 detainment areas that aren't directly linked to the prison system.

Japanese Prisons are bad. The cells are tiny and smell bad. There are no weight rooms or libraries. Gang fights are common. Prisoners get Solitary Confinement. They are often kept from talking to others. The prison is the weakest link in an otherwise strong legal system. They never use Capital Punishment, but prison makes it impossible for anyone to integrate into society. Criminals often stay criminals.

A total of 38 people were shot to death in Japan last year. Most murders are committed with knives or swords. There are lots of arrests, but not an abundant amount of violent crime. You can get up to 15 years for just owning a loaded gun. Compare to 44 people PER DAY who are shot in the US. There have been 12 Subway deaths in Japan since last year. Before that there none. In New York City there are at least 18 people killed on the Subway every YEAR.

The Japanese have very strict gun control. There are only like 49 legal handguns in Japan. Only marksmen or experts are allowed to own them. Shotguns and hunting guns are more common. There are only 425,000 hunting guns in Japan, versus 200 Million guns in the USA. The only illegal guns are tied to the Mafia in Japan.

The Japanese are nervous or afraid to come to the USA to visit as tourists. They see the USA as a dangerous place. They are simply not prepared to deal with so many guns. A Japanese exchange student was shot and killed. He was a kid looking for a party on Halloween night. A husband shot and killed him. That was an accident, but terrorists do target foreign tourist.

Overall, Japan watches less TV than Americans do. They have a higher income and less unemployment than the general American as well. And they live longer!

February 15, 1996 Women and Education

A mother brought her children to her English Class. She believed the need of the kids came first. This is typically a Japanese outlook. Japanese women sometimes talk about how their husbands bring home paycheck, but do not make them happy. It is not easy being "the wife." It is easier, women say, being single.

The average family size is 2.99 people. That is usually just a husband, wife and a single child. Very few families have two children. Population growth has been so slow, the Japanese Government has been encouraging them to have more children. The truth is, most adults are busy taking care of their aging parents and can't afford a ton of children. Only 1 in 20 Japanese will get a divorce vs 1 out of 2 who will get a divorce in the USA. 23% of women work but only 13.5% of these women work full time.

70% of families wanted their son to go to University. But only 30% wanted their daughter to go to the University. However, some 40% of women in Japan do end up going to college now. In the 1970s only 18% of women made it to college.

Student Loans are unusual in Japan. Kids will save for their own own kid's college. Young Japanese workers put back money so they can send their kids to college. A semester at Wooster's Private College here in Ohio s about $18,000 a semester. It is $25,000 a year. In Japan it is $50,000 a year for a private college. It is cheaper at a public University, but not by much in Japan.

Liberal Arts Colleges only take 2 years. Women are more likely to major in English or other Liberal Arts. Men tend to major in Business. There are more openings for men who are college graduates than woman. There is a General College Track that is open to woman and only woman. There are also integrated colleges with both men and woman. Women have to compete with men for good grades and important job openings. Women often have to take a clerical position and work their way up.

In any case, the average woman lives to be 82 years old--the oldest average on the planet. Women do have legal rights and have sued over sexual harassment issues. However, they still have issues with childcare.

Fathers do contribute to housework in Japan. Some 4% of men admit they help their wives with the housework. They average about 21 minutes a day in 1991. That is up from only 12 minutes a day in 1970. 40% of men disagree with the male/female roles. Men don't often have the time to help since work demands all of their time.

Getting a job is not easy. The interviewing process is often very different for women than it is men. The application will often ask for a picture. They ask questions on the application that are considered illegal questions here in the USA. In the interview you might be asked, "Where do you live?" or "Where does your brother or sister work?" Pay is subsidized for singles or married people. Some don't want to hire a single woman. Some of the top questions in 1992 were: "What do you think of Equal Work Laws?" and "How do you combine Work with Family?" and "What are you going to do when you get married" and finally, "How are you going to handle Daycare?"

Many women dropped out of the workforce in the 1980s after they had children. They stay home until their child or children are in school. They work during the day while the kids are in school. They drop out of the work force again after retirement.

Today, during the 1990s, women are dropping out of the workforce less and less. They stay because money is needed. Housing and Education are expensive and they want to help out their children. It is harder to get back into the workforce after being out for a while. They don't want to lose their high paying positions. Women also don't wish to lose their independence. Even still, some women do drop out because family is the most important thing in their lives and they can't take care of the household properly and work full time.

In Japan, women don't want to be exactly like men. They do want equal opportunity. Women find the best solution for them is to work part time. They often find success working as Journalists or Translators.

The Issue of Last Names is an individual decision in the USA. In Japan Names are listed in the Family Register. Generally women take their husband's name. It unusual for a husband to take his wife's name. If a child is illegitimate they can choose their own last name when they turn 20 years old.

February 20, 1996 High School and College Students

Students go to school from 8:30am to 1:30pm Monday thru Friday. On Saturday they go to school from 8:30am Noon. They generally go April through July 20th. They take Summer Vacation from July until September. Second Term meets from October thru December. And 3rd Term is January thru March.

They often eat rice and noodles for lunch since it is cheap. Nearly every student takes part in after school activities. They take music or dance lessons. Some take flower arranging or photography.

Others take Judo or Karate. Soccer and Video Club have increased in popularity.

Students study and cram like crazy so they can get into a Top College. They study Japanese, English, Social Sciences and Natural Sciences in Cram or High School. They get together in the Senior Year before they are too busy studying to get into college.

Very few go to Graduate School. Most finish off with Junior College or a 4 Year College. Not many people have jobs in High School. It is more common in the USA for High Schoolers to have jobs. Very few Japanese quit school. Some might take off a year between High School and College, but not many.

Jobs at Banks are popular for women. The movie showed a lot discussion about the intense pressure to go to college. Boys feel this pressure more than girls. College is just very important. Most parents just want a better life for their children--better than they had at least.

American students study less and watch more TV than Japanese students. The Japanese study a whole day more a week than US students. In the US there are about 175 to 180 days of school. In Japan they go about 240 days a year. They are in school about 4 more years than US students total. This is why Japanese students outperform US students and students around the world. A High School Degree in Japan is equal to a College Degree in the USA. It requires dedication and support from the family's students.

About 75% of students graduate High School in the US, while a full 90% of students graduate in Japan. They have larger classroom sizes. In the US there are 25-30 students, while in Japan there are 40 to 45 students in a classroom. There are less social issues, partly because they wear uniforms all the way into 12th Grade. At least most schools have uniforms. There are some that don't. Usually the uniforms look like they are from the 1920s to the 1950s and they are dark blue or black.

If a family has money, then they have a better chance at getting their kids into a good college. But first they have to have their kids to pass their Kindergarten Exam!

The system is slowly changing though. You have to answer essay questions and get recommendations to get you into good schools. Students outside of Japan were once excluded from the Japanese System. Now foreign students can get into Japanese Schools sometimes. It is really tough though. And some US students graduate without being able to read or write complete sentences.

Now onto Merry White College. In April the College welcomes new students. College is fun. They have a mixture of big and small class sizes. A Quarter of all College students travel. They have part time jobs tutoring at High Schools and other things. They test twice a year. They take Finals and have to write some papers. They take 12 classes that meet once a week. Classes last a year total. Their Senior Year of College they begin their Job Hunt. (Some Students sometimes play Mahjong, which was featured in *The Joy Luck Club*.)

Over half of students don't get into the college of their choice or any college at all. 15% of women go into the Social Sciences. There Women's Colleges and Clubs. These clubs create lifetime friendships. The Skills create ideal leadership schools. Communication skills are incredibly valuable in the work place and in society in general.

Sadly, the US often uses school as a babysitter for kids. They go to school, are bored and then come home and play video games. In Japan, study skills are important. They come home to study and don't watch TV or play video games. Kids in the US struggle to learn a second language, while Japanese students pick up English easily.

February 22, 1996 Review

Key Vocabulary:
Tatenae: means built in front" or "façade" in Japanese
Honne: In Japan, *honne* are a person's true feeling and desires
Yin/Yang: Light and Dark, Male and Female. Harmony and Balance.
Vertical Hierarchy:
Kohai: Junior
Senpai: Senior
Horizontal Relationships: Two friends, brothers, etc.
Duel Structure: Lifetime Employment with Negative and Positive Sides
Enterprise Union: Firm Specific
Miti: Ministry of Industry
Kobans: Police Boxes
Nemawashi: in Japanese means an informal process of quietly laying the foundation for some proposed change or

project, by talking to the people concerned, gathering support and feedback, and so forth.
Women in Work and Education

February 26, 1996 Quiz 3

February 27, 1996 Modern Literature Discussion Kawabata

Personal Matter a novel by Japanese writer Kenzaburō Ōe, which was written in 1964. It won the Nobel Prize. Ōe was born in in 1935. He wrote about Post War Issues. He writes about a son who is mentally retarded. It was a personal matter to decide rather to let the child die or raise it. Society didn't like to deal with the Mentally Handicap. The son was allowed to grow and thrive and he became a talented composer. He is a savant in music and has two CDs available here in the US.

Other Nobel Prize Winners included Yasunari Kawabata in 1968. His first collection of short stories we read. Kawabata lived from 1899 until 1972. He committed suicide in 1972. He died of an overdose.

Categories of Literature:

1) **Very Traditional Japanese** including Kawabata, Yukio Mishimia (Died in 1970) and Tanizaki who wrote *The Makioko Sisters* (1886 to 1965).

2) **The Younger Post-War Generation** who have studied French Literature and others. Kenzaburō Ōe is one of these along with Kobo Abe and Kono Tacko.

3) **The Youngest Generation**: International Haruki Maruakami, Banana Yoshimoto and Japanese British Author **Kazuo Ishiguro** who wrote *The Remains of the Day.*

Style: Think about the Style of Writing of each piece we read. Kawabata writes little dialogues. He captures fleeting feelings. It is impressionistic. Haiku or Waka Poetry is important to him. He is very interested in Nature.

We read 7 Very Short Stories by Kawabata. It was written in 1945 to 1963. We read *"The Second Bravery Attack"* and *"From Elephant Vanishes."* Kawabata also wrote *"Palm of the Hand."* It is one, two, three and four.

1) *Palogrant Tree* that bears brown fruit. He sees a girl. He drops his fruit and it breaks. He sees the seeds and washes the fruit.

He eats the fruit. He thinks of the boy who left for war. He thinks of how mother eats half of things and father eats half of things. The girl carries on the tradition. She gets married to the boy when he comes back. The theme is about the loneliness of war and the beginnings of love. It is about the fruitfulness of life with a poetic style.

2) *Camilla* is about the overpopulation of girls in a particular neighborhood. The story talks of Reincarnation and Miscarriages. There is a folk tale belief that women are a symbol of peace. In New Japan women have rights. After the war there was a baby-boom. The Optimist views life as a cycle of rebirth. He uses the symbol of flowers bursting forth in Spring. Camilla is more like Autumn though. She is old and dying. The narrator wants to find a balance between the optimism of the narrator and the sadness of the character Camilla.

3) *The Plum* is a one page story about a daughter watching her parents grow old. One is senile and the other just had a stroke.

4) *The Jay* was written in 1949. Most authors write bout personal issues. This story is about people writing about people. In Jay a girl lives with her father and step-mother. The son talked to real mothers. The step mothers were often disliked. Families were complicated. Uses the image of a bird falling out of the nest. The mother saved the baby. Was the son the Little Jay?

5) *Summer and Winter* is a story about a not too happy husband. The Husband and wife don't get along. The wife is depressed because the husband thinks she is a failure.

6) *Bamboo Leaves* was written in 1950. It is about a crippled girl who has a limp. She fears losing her fiancée.

7) *The Circus* is about a flower that only blooms for a single evening. It is a cactus flower. The Estranged Husband invites people to come over and see the flower. His daughter is not happy. She thinks he is trying to do some match making.

Snow Country is Kawabata's most famous novel. It was written over a long period of time. Plots are not well developed in the novel. It is a uniquely Japanese novel and is very episodic.

February 28, 1996 Modern Literature Murakami

Murakami lived in Italy and here in the US. He was born in 1949. He studied hard and went to Wasata. He studied Greek and managed a Jazz Bar. He did his writing on the side. He wrote 3 or 4 novels in his spare time. He won awards for his writing and quit working at the Jazz Bar. He was launched as a major literary figure. His work was translated. Eventually he got married and moved.

The Second Bakery Attack had a light tone to it. A husband and wife wake up and hurry to get going. They don't have any food All that is left at their house is beer, onions, butter and air freshener. He is a visualization of hunger. It is like a volcano erupting. He feels like something is absent or missing. She is afraid that the neighbors will think that she is a horrible wife for not having food in the house. The husband tells his friend the story of the Bakery Attack. He didn't want to work, so he stole food. They can't find another bakery to steal from. They find a McDonald's instead. They get 30 Big Macs for the price of one. His emptiness and hunger are physically gone, but not spiritually. Some people read the story as a longing to go back to simpler times before Western Influence.

February 28, 1996 Modern Literature Kono and Yoshimoto

Taeko Kono was born in 1926. *The Last Time* by Kono is what we read first. Is she wasting her last hours on earth? At the end it felt like her marriage wasn't a marriage. It was a real disappointment. She felt like she wasted her life. A real marriage is one where there is struggle, conflict and sharing. She never had children and there were never any secrets. Her husband was selfish and had a drinking problem. He lied about previous wives. Instead of being mad, she related to his other lovers. The notes she leaves are sarcasm and are payback. She does everything around the house. She made dinner and did laundry. Basically she was a doormat. All she could do was worry about her daily routines.

Women's roles were changing in the 1960s. Men's roles were changing, but not nearly as much. Her life was not the most common one. She didn't marry her Painter Husband until age 39. The character is angry and fighting death. At the end she was happy accomplishing

Banana Yoshimoto was born in 1964. We read an excerpt from her novella *Kitchen.* Her novella came out in 1988. We read the first 20 pages or so.

Characters: *Mikage Sakurai is* Young Japanese woman. Main character. Struggling with the loss of her grandmother, who was her last surviving relative. She moves in with Yuichi Tanabe and Eriko

Tanabe after her grandmother's death. ***Yuichi Tanabe*** is the Son of Eriko Tanabe. Main character. His mother died of cancer when Yuichi was a very young child. He lives with his loving transgender mother and supports Mikage in her time of grieving. He eventually loses his mother, and relies on emotional support from Mikage. ***Eriko Tanabe*** is a Supporting character. Transgender woman. Eriko owns a nightclub, which is where she is killed by a man who feels as though she is tricking him by being a transgender woman. She is described as a very beautiful and kind woman.

The main character Mikage loves her Kitchen. It feels the most comfortable. She is lonely since her Grandmother and other family members died. She is physically alone. She had a blanket like Linus from The Peanuts. The book could easily take place in the US as well as Japan. Anyway, she meets a stranger in a flower shop that her Grandmother worked at. He took her in.

March 4, 1996 Slides From Japan

First slide is of the 1972 Olympics. Second slide is of her host family. They were a Dentist and a Doctor and both Upper Class. Jennifer Dell-Ernstrom keeps in contact with her former host family. Next slide is of Ghata or traditional wooden shoes and Raman are instant dry noodles. Next slide is of Hokkaido from Meiji Period, which is being restored. Next slide was Sapporo Snow Festival and an Ice Sculpture in Tajima Hall.

She showed us a middle class house. The father was an English Teacher and the mother was a Secretary. The house was crowded with a tiny garden and steep roofs. The bath is separate from the toilet. Today the Japanese often have a porcelain bowl instead of a toilet. When you enter a house you have to take off your shoes and put on slippers.

Another slide shows the narrow streets of the city on the main island. In Hokkaido, the streets are wider. The kids take public transportation in Hokkaido. We see a slide of a school. There is more than one teacher per school room. The kids stay in one room and the teachers move from room to room. There are lots of rules in schools. Instead of cheerleaders they have cheer boys who chant to the beat of a drum.

Last Slide of a field. There are two crops a year of rice. We talked about how Columbus, Ohio has a Japanese Restaurant called

Sapporo Wind. The Japanese Steakhouse here in Mansfield, Ohio is not authentic.

March 5, 1996 Minorities

Japan is made up of 4% minorities. The biggest group are the Burakumin and are indigenous people. They are left over from the Feudal Society and make up 2-3 million of the population of Japan. Though the Feudal System was abolished, they kept up the same sort of attitudes of the time. Unfortunately, they are often poor and poorly educated. They are discriminated against. Finally, they have become organized and become politically active.

Korean immigrants also live in Japan. The Ainu are Aboriginal. Okinawan are a conquered people. You can't really tell physical difference. Korean and Japanese have a different culture and manor of dress. Many Koreans were made to return to Korea after WWII. In the Northern Providences there are a number of Korean schools. The school uniforms worn by Japanese Schools and Korean Schools are different enough to set them apart. There is still a lot of tension between Korea and Japan. The Japanese feel like they are distinctly different from other Asians.

The Ainu number only around 50,000. They are equivalent to the Native Americans. They were pushed further northward up into Hokkaido. The Modern Japanese conquered them. The Ainu look different. Some even have blue eyes. The have more body hair than other Japanese. They have no written language and no tribal lands.

Okinawa is South of the Mainland. It is far away from the Ainu in the North. It is grouped closer to Thailand and China. There are 78 islands, but only 48 are inhabitable. It has a subtropical climate. It's hilly lands were invaded by the Japanese in 1872. The Islands had been their own kingdom with it's own King. They paid tribute to China until Japan took over.

During WII there was a 3 month battle that raged over the island. The US Military took it over and occupied it. Now there is a US Military Base there. Okinawa developed tourism after 1972. They have resorts like Hawaii. The average income is lower in Okinawa than the mainland. Big Hotel and Tourism has helped. However, the people of Okinawa hold resentment over American Occupation. Much of the crime committed in Okinawa is on the Military bases.

To become a Japanese Citizen you must have a Japanese Mother or Father. If the mother is not Japanese and the father denies it's his, then the baby would not get citizenship. You can live in Japan for 3 years as long as you behave. If you have any run-ins with the law that hurts the Japanese or Chinese, you can get kicked out. You have carry registration and ID. You go to the police station and get fingerprinted. They often use colorless ink that is less humiliating than black.

East Asians may have mixed marriages, but they are often discriminated against. Half white and Half Japanese are less discriminated against than Half Korean and Half Japanese. Half white and half Filipino or Vietnamese are discriminated against the most. Kids refer themselves as doubles not halves. There are very few Africans in Japan.

March 7, 1996 Review for Final
March 11, 1996 Final

African Art and Archaeology
History of Art 216

Instructor: Mrs. Diane Alemendinger
Office: Ovalwood 379
Meetings: Tuesdays and Thursdays
Spring 1996

Course Objective: For the Student to have an understanding of the art and archaeology related to Mali, Ghana, The Cameroon, The Congo and Nigeria. The Art of the Dogon, The Bambara, The Ashanti, The Dan, The Yoruba and Others. The goal of this course a strong enough knowledge of the material to be able to match each piece of art to the tribe that made it.

Required Text: *African Art and Archaeology* OSU Workbook, 1995
Things Fall Apart by Chinua Achebe, 1994
Return to Laughter: An Anthropological Novel, Eleanor Smith Bowen, February 20, 1964

March 25, 1996 Introduction

We need to be able to identify what tribe made what piece of art for the exam. We will also need to know what the name of the artwork and its function. We will read the OSU Workbook African Art and Archaeology as well as three novels for the class.

Our teacher wanted to go to Africa. She thought Tarzan was good looking and she loved that he didn't wear shoes. Alemendinger realized it was important to wear shoes in Africa though she would get an infection. In *A Return to Laughter* the author found three pair of shoes necessary. Tribes thought she was rich.

Many African tribes have a Rite of Passage. Most tribes do not have a written language. They speak their native language or a Colonial Language. French, German, Italian and English are spoke in various African Countries. In Somalia paper is so rare that they are forced to memorize things.

Food is very different over there. Stews are common. Peanuts are a good source of protein since they don't always have access to meat. We will get a chance to choose an Africa Dish to cook and share with the class at the end of the Quarter.

Africa is the oldest Continent above Sea Level. The earliest remains of humans have been found in East Africa—aka Lucy. At one time all the continents were a single continent named Pangaea. All of the continents moved around and drifted away. Africa stayed in the same place since the formation of the continents.

West Africa doesn't really have a good coast line though. You can't swim the ocean there due to really strong undercurrents. Africa is like a saucer. It is higher on the coast and dips down in the center. It also has 5 really large lakes and the Nile that flows through it. The Nile and other rivers look like brown snakes running through the green and brown landscapes. Around each bend in the rivers you will find a different group, tribe or village.

The concept of land ownership is different in Africa. Whoever owns land has supreme power. If they own it, then they have to take care of it. They do sometimes use the slash and burn method, but rarely. Most tribes are good environmentalist.

Respect is important. To the Muslim community photos of people's faces are bad. The left hand is unclean because they wipe themselves with it. The Chief of a tribe will show respect by touching his forehead to the ground and sits on his knees.

West Africa and Central Africa are our primary area of study. East Africa has more mobile people. They follow cattle herds across large lengths of land. The Watose who live there wear their art. Traditional African Art is divided into the various tribes and their geographical locations. In North Africa there are the Blue Men of the Desert or the Berbers. In South Africa there was a group called the Hot and Tots, but the Dutch who settled there killed them all. South Africa has been the site of much conflict since the White Settlers arrived. The White Settlers were called New Africans.

The Weather in West Africa is normally hot and dry. When it rains, it pours so hard it tears open the cloth umbrellas. Along the coast there is a nice cool sea breeze and you might need a jacket in the evenings. Social life included carrying an oil lamp to go talk to people in the evening. Ms. Alemendinger had to wear a skirt and T-shirt. She couldn't wear jeans or shorts for fear of being labeled a prostitute. She also had to take soap with her. Deodorant consisted of half of a lemon and half of a lime. Toothbrushes are basically just a chew stick.

Memphis Middle School is in Ghana starts at 8am. At noon they would break for lunch. Mostly they eat Rice for lunch. At 2 o'clock they cut grass with a machete to great rid of all the snakes. The Palm tree that is common in the area is not good wood to build with. They go to North Ghana to get better wood to build with. They use wood from the baobab tree. They burn the inside of of the trunk and then carve the rest out with a sharp stick. They need to build two strong fishing canoes that can hold 20 men. They also need two strong swimmers to pull the nets back in after they finished fishing. Pulling the nets in can pull the skin off their hands. It is hard work.

Further down the river they gather millet or grain. Villages send people to other villages to marry. It isn't good to marry someone from your own village because there is a chance of incest or health problems do to interbreeding. The fishing villages trade with the villages inland and so they get a chance to meet other people outside of their own villages.

Fonte is the name of the fishing village. A girl gets married to someone from the farming village. The dowry is a beaded belt. The Groom's family gives goats to the bride's family. Divorce is possible, but the family must give back the dowry. Africans recognize umbilical hernia and think it is desirable among girls because it keeps them connected their mothers.

The soil of West Africa is nearly pure iron. The Missionaries brought in farming tools, but their tractors often got stuck. Now villages know how to use fertilizers and such. However, they still leave gardens alone. They share their gardens with animals and don't worry about putting up fences.

Women do the farming in Africa. They carry heavy loads on their heads, necks and backs. They are very strong. A long handled hoe hurts the back. A short handled hoe is better.

It 700 AD Muslims came from the North and descended into Africa. They went to **Timbuktu.** It became a center of trade, including trading slaves. While the slave trade wasn't a good thing, the Muslims or Arabs brought reading and writing with them. The Merchants there were the middlemen between wealthy Saudi Arabians and the buyers in Africa. The Saudi Arabians knew the world was round and had maps that showed it. In 1441 Europeans made their way to Timbuktu as well.

Ghana's chief is now one of 300 Paramount Chiefs. The Primary Chief has solid gold clothes. The metal is formed in wax and gold is poured through a tube into empty spaces. They used narrow strips to weave as well. The Muslims brought salt and to trade for humans and for ivory.

Slavery existed within Africa. It could be benevolent slavery when a witch is exiled into a village. Sometimes you can marry out of slavery and become a member of a new tribe. Men caught as prisoners of war were used and sold as slaves. They were considered less than human. There were slave fortresses or castles. Men and women were held separately. They were held for three months and then taken out to ships in canoes.. They were chained together to keep them from running and drowning.

Africans are very religious. Art is ritual. Dogon's God is Amah. Spirituality comes from lightening. It is very powerful and invisible. The creative force created the Dogon's tribe first. Their geographical location is very important. They keep shrines to renew religious belief. Ritual and Art are intermingled. Clay figures are magical to the Dogon.

Tribe members are born into a particular position. In one group you might laugh at the elders while in another group you act all serious and respectful. Process is more important than the project. Men have to carve a mask worn while in bush schools. Magic is a process. Sometimes they crawl into a cave to paint a vision into a picture. Magic is about mental or spiritual growth and transitions. It also helps them gain power within the tribe or village.

In 1441 the Portuguese landed on the coast of West Africa. Missionaries burned the wooden statues that they found. Statutes are not graven images. They are tributes to the ancestors. They are a container for the spirit. They won't have a funeral until 3 years after the death. The whole village is fed at the funeral. While preparing for the funeral, the spirit will be contained in the wooden statue. Loved ones will speak to the spirit in the statue. The spirit stays happy during this time as long as people pay attention to it. If the villagers don't keep the spirit happy then it may come back and steal the children due to being lonely.

Most of the religion or philosophy is centered on trying to keep control of their environment. It is a group effort. So, to be exiled is the worst punishment. People believe they can die from witchcraft or curses from a witch-doctor. On the flip side, witch-doctors can also give spells and potions to heal illness. Owls are symbolic of witches.

Seeing an owl will prompt one to find out who is working witchcraft against them. They will go buy a white hen and bathe it. Then they give the white chicken someone who doesn't have one. The afflicted will drink the water the chicken bathed in. This was a prescription given from a witch-doctor to Alemendinger's daughter.

Witch Doctors used clay and metal rings. They would dress up with the horns of animals on their heads. They would wear braided grass on their clothing. Witch Doctors used a Divination tray to predict the future. They would read bones and other objects on the tray in much the same way others read tea leaves or tarot cards.

Africa is where the humans evolved. It is the location of our genesis. It is the oldest continent where humans have lived. It is here the heart of human evolution that art evolved as well. There is no word for art there though. Art is divorced from the object. All art is magical. It is not only decorative, but a vital part of life as well.

Family groups create clans. These clans grow into villages and a group of villages becomes a Kingdom. They have a form of King-ship, but it is not like European Monarchies. Rank of a member in the clan, village or kingdom is shown by clothes worn and art owned.

Art has changed in Africa with the arrival of Christians and Muslims. Early tribal art was all about animism. The art was a living part of their world. Christians changed their perception of art from living to symbolic. People in Africa have not been SHAPED by Europe, but RE-SHAPED by them. The people in Africa had complex societies, religions, government, rules and law. They were not heathen savages like they were painted to be

Need to know these terms:

Rites de Passage: French for Rites of Passage.
Prestige: Fame
Scarification: Scarring for the Rites of Passage
Shaman: Is a Witch-Doctor, Priest, and Healer
Divination: Being or Making Divine
Bride Price: Dowry
Animism: Interrelated with Nature, Nature is Alive and Conscious

March 27, 1996 Art of the Sundanese Belt: The Dogon

Mrs. Alemendinger played some Africa music for us. "*Dun Da Da Da Ta Aha*" There is one string harp, flutes, drums and a voice. There are no brass instruments. They have rhythm from hips, knees, shoulders and feet. They will stomp, jump or move side to side to the music.

One person in the tribe was a designated an important historian or Griot (pronounced Greo). He keeps the tribe's history in his mind. He then tells others. He is like a bard. Halley's went to a Griot in his ancestor's tribe. Griot sang his story and it connected back to Halley's Comet. The bard has license to insult even a tribal chief when he is singing the story of their history. The Griot is like glue. He holds people together with the knowledge of the tribe. He is their history and their identity.

Alemendinger explained that growing up in Africa is very different from growing up in the USA. The average income is $200 a year. Now it is $400 a year. Every family is responsible for everyone in the family. Some in Sierra Leon only make $6 a year. The prostitute makes more than farmers. They are often burdened with unwanted children though. In Western Africa an effort has been made to keep the water clean, etc. Not all African countries have it as good.

Houses are made with mud and wattle. Bamboo or wood is interlocked with mud and wattle. These create brick. They build their houses in the dry season with these bricks. The roofs are thatched. Often there are chickens, goats and dogs hanging out around homes. They fend for themselves and are not fed by the people who live there. They will even eat the dogs if they need food. They use goats for milk and don't eat them very often. More likely the goat will be sacrificed.

SLIDES: Girls at 3 months old begin learning how to be wives and mothers. Boys learn to be warriors, husbands and fathers.

Art commemorates rites of passage and secret societies. Some countries practice genital mutilation or the cutting off of the clitoris. The UN has been trying to get this barbaric practice outlawed. Girls will go into shock. The may even die of blood loss.

Men undergo scarification. The skin is sliced open and wood ash is sprinkled in. It welts up and scars. The wood ash keeps them from bleeding to death often times. The scars show knowledge and wisdom. Boys will also go to Bush School every three years. They go for the first time when they are very little. The second time they are a bit older. The third time they are teens and it is their final time. Scarification is seen as marking the rite of passage and is found attractive by others in their society.

Missionaries convinced them to scar the statues instead of themselves. Then they destroyed the statues. Scarification does still happen in some places. As for the statues, it is difficult to find pieces before the Colonial Period. Yoruba make Leopard Paw Scars. A lot of people from Nigeria (Yoruba) traveled to England. They are easily recognizable since they are often tall and stately.

Some Africans have no hair on their arms. Men will not have facial hair. Women don't have to shave their legs, etc. Women often wear extensions in their hair. They also braided and wrapped their hair. Hairdos were considered works of Art.

Women are eligible for marriage after their first period. Marriages are often arranged between villages for economic reasons. The villages are dependent on each other. The single girls are paraded around on their brother's shoulders. Scars are put on display. The husband's family may sing or say insults to her in an effort to scare her away. The girl will be put in her future husband's hut. If she cries, she will be sent back along with her bride price--goats or whatever. If there is competition for a girl there will be a wrestling match or foot race or something. Older men often marry younger women. The girls will begin bearing children as soon as they are able.

Children are wealth. Some women don't have to work while pregnant and they are kept separate from the rest of the village. Then they go back home to give birth. A woman who has a difficult pregnancy or delivery may be suspected of having a lover or something. Lovers are not unheard of in a society where marriage is mostly a contract and not done out of love. However, women who cheat are treated very poorly compared to men who cheat. In any case, the midwife's nickname Tommy.

Baby names are often based on the day of the week they were born and then the family name. The mother pretends that she is not interested in her child for the first three months. They are instructed to not let the child know how much you love them. Why? Probably because it will break the mother's heart if the baby dies. If a baby lives to 3 months, they will have a naming ceremony. A mother will breastfeed for 2 years and then the baby will go straight to adult food.

The mother can abstain from sex for up to three years. Depending on where they live or the circumstances of their marriage, sometimes the man will have an affair or take a second wife. Women aren't usually allowed to have affairs, except if her husband is old and unable to give her a baby. If a man marries other women, the first wife or Senior Wife will choose the Junior Wives.

We watched the First part of the Movie *Roots*. It was accurate in showing babies without diapers and women who didn't wear any sort of rag or cloth for menstruation. The movie runs through the names of the family. The baby is held up in the moonlight and urinates. The urine is a sign of his name. He knows his ancestor has been reborn. It is a circular sort of reincarnation. Souls are immortal unless they commit some sort of taboo.

Back to our discussion: The second wife will then go through pregnancy and childbirth. The older children are responsible for the younger children. There are Children as young as 4 years old will be in charge of babies. They may carry their younger brother or sister on their hip. Boys as will go to bush school together even if they are 4 year apart.

We learn twins are important to his ancestors. The multiple wives share the work. How does she mark time? She goes to market every 5 to 7 days. It is an important thing that women do. Men are not included. She will see other women from her village there. It is a social affair. There are some cows in Africa. Mostly they buy canned milk from the market. She may buy sweet balls, which are similar to donuts. She may also buy boiled peanuts in a leaf and hot peppers. Cleanliness is important with the market and food preparation. The bus the women travel in is an old station wagon.

Palm wine is also available. They drain the sap from the palm tree and distill it. Palm wine is like hard cider. Everyone drinks it and they drink from the same dipper. They also only eat two meals a day because food takes so long to prepare and cook. Foo Foo is food. White yams are tubers that are dug up and eaten. It is a large potato, although it doesn't particularly taste like a potato.

Africans frequently walk long distances. They wear flip flops or sandals and may carry very heavy loads. Women may trade firewood for jeans. When they reach the agreed upon place, they sometimes say, "Yahoo, are you there?"

Children may walk a long way just to go to school. Education is now required, but it wasn't compulsory for a long time. During

Colonial times they taught the names and dates of English Kings.
They also taught and still teach the English Language.

The Great Chief will bow down and get dust on his forehead.
Africans claim they invented the folding chair. Wives wore the same
cloth as husband to identify their chief. In the 1980s people bought
clothes made in Africa. The Dutch introduced a lot of the cloth used
in their modern clothing. African Art was brought to the US and
other places in the 1980s as well.

A tailor came with her own sewing machine and made a dress fro
Alemendinger. It was plain with some embroidery. It took three days
and only cost $5.

THE DOGON

The Dogon have the *Myth of the Red Fiber Skirt* and the *Myth of
the Egg of World* are important to know. But first we will discuss
who the Dogon are. They live in Mali, an area that is South of
Timbuktu and is pretty remote. They traveled in a caravan to
Morocco and Egypt. The Muslims have influenced the Dogon.
Muslims took young Dogon to use as slaves in their Harems or sold
them at Timbuktu. The Dogon eventually abandoned Timbuktu. It
was a difficult place to live and there was little water. The Dogon
have an epic poem that outlines their history.

The Myth of the Egg of the World: *"In the beginning, Amma
(God), alone, was in the shape of an egg: the four collar bones were
fused, dividing the egg into air, earth, fire, and water, establishing
also the four cardinal directions. Within this cosmic egg was the
material and the structure of the universe, and the 266 signs that
embraced the essence of all things. The first creation of the world by
Amma was, however, a failure. The second creation began when
Amma planted a seed within herself, a seed that resulted in the
shape of man. But in the process of its gestation, there was a flaw,
meaning that the universe would now have within it the possibilities
for incompleteness.*

*Now the egg became two placentas, each containing a set of
twins, male and female. After sixty years, one of the males, Ogo,
broke out of the placenta and attempted to create his own universe,
in opposition to that being created by Amma. But he was unable to
say the words that would bring such a universe into being. He then
descended, as Amma transformed into the earth the fragment of*

placenta that went with Ogo into the void. Ogo interfered with the creative potential of the earth by having incestuous relations with it. His counterpart, Nommo, a participant in the revolt, was then killed by Amma, the parts of his body cast in all directions, bringing a sense of order to the world.

When, five days later, Amma brought the pieces of Nommo's body together, restoring him to life, Nommo became ruler of the universe. He created four spirits, the ancestors of the Dogon people; Amma sent Nommo and the spirits to earth in an ark, and so the earth was restored. Along the way, Nommo uttered the words of Amma, and the sacred words that create were made available to humans. In the meantime, Ogo was transformed by Amma into Yuguru the Pale Fox, who would always be alone, always be incomplete, eternally in revolt, ever wandering the earth seeking his female soul."

The Millet Grass seed plants itself. The seeds explode in a spiral. It is said it is Yuguru springing from the world.

A Hogon is a Dogon Spiritual Leader or Witch Doctor. The Dogon blacksmith is kind of like a middle man or priest. Since a blacksmith can change metal, he is revered and feared. He brings the heavens to earth. Blacksmith daughters will marry Blacksmith sons from other villages.

April 1, 1996 Dogon *"Behind The Mask"*

The Dogons wanted to escape the Muslim slave trade, so they left Timbuktu on a Journey. Mali 5 went 5 years without a drop of rain. Women had to walk really far for water. They made elaborate carvings, but the white ant destroyed most of them. Then the Dogon discovered short Red Men living in caves in Mali. It is thought these short Red Men were aboriginals and that the Dogon were Black Invaders in the area. These Red Men were called "Bushmen" and forced to migrate to what is now Zaire.

The Dogon respected the Little Red Bushmen. The Dogon were taught by the Red Bushman how to circumcise and other things. They were taught their funeral rites as well. The Tellum statue with hands above its head celebrates these things. The statues can be either sex. Some have both sexes in one, representing the soulmate twin. Some statues will feature lip plugs. Others may feature an extended stomach signifying pregnancy.

The Dogon have use caves to bury the dead. They lives in houses with a pointed roof. Where they have sacred spaces, they put round houses. The houses are made from mud with branches of trees to reinforced. They have terrace houses, which are the center of their social lives. They sleep out under the stars to clear their consciences.

They also fill granary and distribute it. The granary has a special door to represent Nammo. The door keeps the rats out. On the door we see twin snakes called Lebe that bring immortality. Crocodiles are often depicted since they help them cross the river. These doors go for $300 for a replica and $50,000 for an original. In any case, they use the grain to make beer. Millet Beer is quite important to the Dogon. They pour it over the cones of the holy buildings. The birds eat the also millet but it doesn't taste too good. Millet hay is used to thatch their roofs.

The only way to activate a sacred mask is to touch it to the Mother Mask. There are 80 styles of masks. The Dogon sell their art these days. The Dogon have the most abstract art in the ancient world. In fact, Picasso studied their artwork and came up with Cubism using their work as a template. They use recognizable shapes, but don't worry about realistic details. Their artwork pair male and females together as symbolism for the great ancestors. They are often shown with the female putting her arm around the male. These statues are about 4 feet tall! In any case, the Twin Nummo is older than anyone and the Dogon show respect for him.

They continue to worship Amma, but it is one of the poorest countries in the world. The Dogon fought the French during WWII. They still have some flint lock guns from that era.

They trade green onions for other things. Although women are the ones who farm, it is the men who make the laws. The men have councils and hold meetings in houses. The onion is commonly found there, but it is also symbolic of their many layered world. Each layer reflects the good and the bad. Onions and everything in the world has defects. These defects make them closer to the divine.

Kanaga is the Funeral Dance and the use a special wooden mask for it. It is a death mask that is associated with a red fiber skirt. Men will wear the mask with a hood and the red fiber skirt. These masks are huge. They try to duplicate or replicate the spiral of coming to the earth and hitting the ground.

Paris has a large Dogon art exhibit. Texas also has a decent display of Dogon art. The Cleveland Museum of Art has a few pieces. You can also find exhibits at Natural History Museums.

This episode of *The Tribal Eye* (1975) entitled "*Behind The Mask"* centers on the life and customs of the Dogon people in Mali, concentrating primarily on their masks and mask rituals. After a brief introduction to the Dogon culture, the link between African and European art is elaborated upon, using works by Picasso and Braque as examples. Dogon blacksmiths are shown working on a sculpture and a monkey mask for an old woman's funeral; the funeral rites, which include masked performances and a staged mock battle, are shown in great detail.

The movie begins by discussing Divination. The wise man draws symbols in the sand or dirt. A fox runs over the symbols and then the wise man reads the changed drawings. The fox tracks will tell the future. The Hogon is like the village priest. A special few see the art in the Dogon society. Special pieces are often hidden. The Hogon are said to come from heaven. They wear iron sandals to keep the ground sterile. They look at the water that creates pools in the rocks.

Onions are ground into a mush and then molded into balls to dry. This is millet and their basic food. The Hogon is an intermediary. The Blacksmith, Artist, Magician, Warrior and Priest come to him. They sing and use plates to making a clicking noise. They paint symbols on rocks and conduct Bush Schools, which are like secret societies.

Awa is the Society of Masks. It is a Secret Society. Every boy makes his own mask. When they are done, they bring the masks down from the Bush school and dance. There are strips of rock that are dangerous. They aren't allowed to step on these rocks.

The Tribal Eye Episode talks about the Cowie Shell. It is buried beneath a tree as an offering. They boy will take a limb from that tree to carve the mask. The Bush Master keeps track of all the masks. He knew who is allowed to wear what. He allows the maker of the mask to wear it, but never near the rocks. They paint the masks black with vegetable oil or sap. The Sculptures are not ornamental. It is religious. There is no word for Art in Dogon. Is it correct? The mask speaks truth. That is what is important, not if it is beautiful, good or perfect. The masks are paraded through the night. The men become heroes from the past. The masks have become spirits from the other world. The Bull Roar or Bowl Rorah's signal the end of the night.

April 3, 1996 The Dogon "*The Dark Star*" and The Bambara

Dogon religious life is heightened every 60 years by a ceremony called the *sigui*, which occurs when the star Sirius appears between two mountain peaks. Before the ceremony, young men go into seclusion for three months, during which they talk in a secret language. The general ceremony rests on the belief that some 3,000 years ago amphibious beings from Sirius visited the Dogon.

In Kenya all young boys carve this death mask for a funeral during their first contact with Awa. Not all boys dance in the Kenyan dance though. Kenya is in East Africa, which is more tourist friendly. The Airport has butterfly art and a carved giraffe, etc. The Ant Hill is a symbol for mother earth. Feminine is finer than sand.

All beings have carved women as they look in their prime, which is about 35 years old. They often are portrayed as having fuller breasts. Sometimes they are portrayed with skinny rabbit masks. There is also a sacred container that is made that contains meat. That meat is only used by the Hogon. It is a diamond shaped container with snakes and water on it. A mule or horse will adorn the cover. They will sacrifice goats and chickens and hold the meat in the container while serving it.

The Myth of the Red Fiber Skirt: Myths help with problem solving skills, etc. This myth explains why the Dogon wear a red skirt. There is a correlation between the Little Red Men. Death is seen as unnatural. We are meant to live forever and be immortal.

There is an 800-verse poem that included The Myth of the Red Fiber. The Red Fiber Skirt was created for Mother Earth to hide her sex. She had sex with her son Yuguru, who is known as the Fox or the jackal. The Fibers are made red with Menstruation blood. They are laid out in the sun to dry. The skirt is used to celebrate the little red men and women who were needed to create the red skirt. To wear the Red Fiber Skirt honors the Dead who did not die until they were infected by the first red fibers.

We watched A& E Show *In Search Of.* Season 4 Episode 13 from 1979, which is titled "*The Dark Star.*" (The Dark Star: Travel to Africa to find out why the **Dogon**, a primitive tribe knows so much about **astronomy**, a **black hole**, and travelers from outer space.) Dr. Hans Guggenheim lived for 5 years with the Dogon. He learns about The Dark Star, known as Sirius B, Leonard Nimoy narrates.

The Dark Star was identified by Astronomers for the first time in 1950. The Dogon somehow knew about it a long time before that. Their story about how the plates were thrown out and the egg collapsed parallel the process of Sirius B collapsing.

All Human activity is involved in weaving. The original mask celebrating the journey of Sirius is over 300 years old. How did they know? Can the Dingi or Dogon see into the Universe? Do they have ESP? Did Aliens visit them? Are they descended from Aliens? The fact that blood circulates throughout the body was known to them before the English knew it. Nummo landed on Earth in Egypt. Did the Pyramids guided him to that spot?

Skirts are now sometimes dyed with chemicals. The Dutch East Indies Trading Company brought brightly colored cloth with them. Black, Brown and Red are the colors that are typically used.

Bambara or Bamana live in Mali. They were there after the Dogon left. They live in the neck area of Mali and were heavily influenced by the Muslims. Today they make up the largest Mandé West African ethnic group in Mali, with 80% of the population speaking the **Bambara language**, regardless of ethnicity.

The masks that the Bambara create vary from group to group. Sometimes the mask just covers the front of the face, while some cover just the forehead and others the whole head. Bambara wear them on the top of the head mostly. The males and females dance together. They will have a little hat on top of the mask and sometimes goat horns. The go through N'tomo or the Secret Society of the Uncircumcised. Then they go through Kore or a sexual organization. There is also Nama, Kono and Chi Wara for males. Chi Wara is the highest level that can be reached. They become a hero if they reach that level.

The do their dances in the Spring and Fall. They go into the Bush for the first time when they are five. The foreskin of the penis is considered feminine. The Clitoris is considered masculine and must be removed. Every male is given a female counterpart. You can marry your counterpart and you can't have sex with them. They are like your twin. The male is responsible for protecting the female and making sure that she is still a virgin when she is married.

The Cosmological Myth of the Bambara: Power comes from the heavens. Faro is the name of their god. Humans were already here. They were farmers who weren't doing well. They were wasting grain, so he calls upon a divine creature to be born from a woman and a snake. Chi Wara was the name of that offspring and he came in the form of the antelope. Faro gave humans consciousness and responsibility. They were finally able to administer justice among them. Chi Wara was able to help the Bambara learn how to farm well. He gave them Sun Sticks. The Dance of Chi Wara is the dance of the male and female. The Sun Sticks are transformed into Maize. These magical sticks mean prosperity and fertility.

Then men grew lazy once again. Chi Wara was disappointed in men. He digs a hole and goes into it. Chi Wara is reincarnated, so to speak. He comes back in the form of the Boli, the most sacred container. The House of Chi Wara means all sorts of souls in the village can go into the Boli when they die. The Dance of Chi Wara is done twice a year in April or May and then again in October. Boli is a stone with four sticks tied to it. Mud, blood and Millet is made into plaster. It can be as big as a dog and has a crusty cover.

The men return Bambara for an from the Tropical Rubber Plantations in October. Segoni Kun is the name of the mask going around the room right now. It was made by a Chi Wara dance. Artists in Bambara are also blacksmiths. They are not segregated occupations like in the Dogon society.

The oldest men and women carry headdresses out to the field and bring Boli along the path to the field of the dance. Women musicians sing and clap, but they don't dance. The women first pass over the Boli. The best housewife has to get all her chores done before she can rest. She makes a box lunch for her man or her assigned twin. Men hid in the field and when the women arrive, they come out of the field. The men stab each other with a hot coal, but it doesn't hurt. Women balance the Boli on a spear. The first woman of the group will give the best dancer lunch.

April 8, 1996 The Bambara and Senufo

Bambara are infidel. It is the Muslim word for those who don't pray. The 16th Century Caravans arrived. It was rumored that the Bambara Chief ate off a golden plate, but they did not know how to work bronze or other metals.

In **Bambara**, *chi wara* means *laboring wild animal* and is a representation of Bambara Mythos about the creation of farming. The Chi Wara itself is usually represented as a Roan Antelope with an almost human face, but also takes shapes of other creatures and emblems of farming. The hero descends from the sky goddess, and thus represents the sun, its body is often elongated and short legged to represent the **aardvark** who burrows into the earth like a farmer. Its high horns echo the stalks of **millet**, and it stands on a dancer clad in a mass of **raffia** stalks to represent both flowing water and a bountiful harvest. The zig-zag patterns echo the movement of the sun across the sky, and the penis of the male figure stands low to the ground, fertilizing the earth. The Chi Wara figures always appear as a male/female pair, combining the elements of fertility of humans with fertility of the earth. The female figure usually carries a young antelope on her back, and is said to represent human beings carried by the Chi Wara hero, as well as a newborn human carried on a mother's back.

There are vertical and horizontal masks. The ones with Vertical Antlers are made with Antelope Antlers. The Chiwara can be used to dig soil. The Muslims influenced the open neck of the Chiwara. Vertical Masks require two men to dance. The Horizontal Masks belong to the Best House Wife or their Gender Twin. One of the Masks looks like an Elephant or Snuffleupagus. The Highest Rank of dancer is the Chiwara. Lots of Interior Decorators use African Art, specifically Bambara Horizontal Masks.

The early Muslims were animists. They believed everything was alive or had a soul. This meant the masks had a life of their own as well. Animals were thought to have human qualities. The Anasi Trickster Spider Legend of Ghana traveled to the Caribbean and up through the South. It became the Legend of Brer Rabbit.

Anyway, the Atoma is the Mother of Circumcision. The Atoma mask has 3 to 8 Horns and is plain or covered in Seeds and/or Cowie shells. Atoma mask has a female figure on top. Her breasts are cone shaped and her hands are flat.

Komo Masks are the Highest Ranking. They are representative of a Water Spirit and treated as human. The mask is buried when the human it belongs to dies. Gwan (nickname) is important to women. Each figure has a Gwan figure. Women pray to the Gwan that they will be fertile. The figure has hair tied in three pig tails and is seated on a stool with a baby on her lap. Sometimes the Gwan figure has a pregnant belly instead of a baby. Gwan means something beautiful to look at.

African Art has a 1/3rd division. 1/3 of the statue is the head. 1/3 is the reproductive organ and 1/3 is the legs. Some 95% of African Art is Frontal. That is the figure faces the front, but the back is often flat. The Bambara figures have feet, unlike the Dogon figures

The Mud Cloth is very popular. The dye is made from boiled bark or leaves. They sometimes use iron in their paint. They will washout or beat out the mud. The cloth will be stained with brown, black or white patterns. Men wear this for good luck in hunting and warfare.

The Senufo are located between Mali and the Ivory Coast. The Ivory Coast's capital is Abjon and is a French Territory. The country has a very poor population and has a Catholic Church there. The President taxed everyone to build the expensive church even though it was only for a small congregation. The Pope came to make the ground consecrated. Only 10% of The Ivory Coast is actually Catholic though. It costs roughly $3,950 to fly to the Ivory Coast in 1996.

The Senufo don't like to be photographed in general. They feel it is rude and have superstition around it. Some believe it can capture one's soul.

There are children and old people in the village. Young adults go out and work in the fields. The soil has a lot of iron in it, so it is a reddish color. They live in round houses with thatched roofs. The men's houses are a lot like the Dogon. The big roofs make the building cooler. Men make the policy in the Senufo tribes. Dogs are often sacrificed.

You will see stone with patterns embedded in them. They make naked mud figures as well as serpents and other animals. The figures will watch the doors of their home. They make the figures to honor those who could bless the fertility of their fields and human women.

The Figure they make is called the Deble. They are rhythm pounders with a figure and a flat bottom for pounding the ground. The dance partners go to the sight of the dance and dampen down the dance area in the sacred grove. The pound their feet and pack the mud. It connects them the dead beneath them.

The Senufo figures have a far out chin and mouth which come to a point. Their mouth is shaped like it is whistling. They have very muscular, Popeye-like, arms. On the head of the figure is a diadem or crown. The Egyptians also made figures with diadems. There are also rows of grooves. Some figures have bound hands and a carved out hands. There are horn-bill figures that look like the bill of a bird.

There are also scorpion masks or masks with scorpions carved into them.

In the Senufo tribe it is believed that men can't touch menstrual blood. They leave that they will lose their powers if they do. The males have their own secret society and it is the largest of the West Coast. Poro is the name of it and they regulate men's activities throughout Liberia, Ivory Coast and Gambia.

Ma'T is the concept leader. He is a benevolent person and a care-taker. He is the Good Shepherd. The Kerchief that Ma'T wears is connected to Egypt as well.

In Senufo Villages all women are potters. They collect clay and create pots and other things. They also are gardeners and farmers. They kneed the clay with their feet. They don't have a potter's wheel to work with. The pots walls are thin. You can pick it up with hand usually. If the women do not make it perfectly, then the teacher smashes it. They burn the pots in the fire for three hours.

They grow carrots, lettuce, peas and yams. There isn't much food. The people in the villages lack iron and often suffer from goiter.

Kopeli Masks are another thing that is made. It is a mask with a heart-shaped face. Its eyes are nearly closed and they look serene. The mouth is open and it shows its teeth. It goes along with Symbols of the Moon. Two older men teach another single younger man. They teach him the concept of duality. There is the Sun and Moon as well as Day and Night. There is Good and Evil or Light and Dark. Some Masks reflect this dual nature with a double face.

The Kopeli Dance happens when they gather under the trees. Musicians brings bronze gongs. They hit them with a mallet and call the spirits forth. A flute plays and a sort of ballet corps come out of the bush. Boys without masks dance wildly in their grass skirts. The best dancer practically loses his mind in the frenzy. Women wear the same prints as the dancers, but they sit on the sidelines and sing. Nowadays dancers can get a boom box and record the music so they can practice. Older tribe members chastise or yell at the younger dancers for doing this.

April 10, 1996 Senufo, Baga and Mende

The *Sandogo* are women diviners among the Senufo people. They have their own rituals and secret order. In addition, the Senufo people have *Wambele* and *Typka,* who perform sorcery and rituals. A woman will pay another woman with cowrie shells or coins and ask her to read the future. Is the woman going to be lucky in love? She sends love potions in gourds. The potions require hair and nail clippings of the desired.

The Regionally, the Senufo are famous as musicians and superb carvers of wood sculpture, masks, and figurines. The Senufo people have specialized their art and handicraft work by subgroups, wherein the art is learned within this group, passed from one generation to the next. The *Kulubele* specialize as woodcarvers.

The Kulubele masks have heart-shaped faces. Their chin jets out. Lips will look like the face is whistling. If it is a female figure she will have pointed breasts. Senufo people put arms, hands, legs and feet on their figures. Sometimes they are shaped like animals. Sometimes the Kulubele has two figures or faces. Screen Masks are young initiates into their society. Some of these Screen Masks are 4 feet tall. Other figures are on horses.

The masks are hidden in a secret grove in a room. The dancer get the masks and will hold a container of cinders. They dance at night. There are sometimes fire-spitters. They may have horse races or carving contests in addition to the dances.

The *Fonombele* specialize in blacksmith and basketry work, the *Kpeembele* specialize in brass casting, the *Djelebele* are renowned for leather work, the *Tchedumbele* are masters of gunsmith work, while *Numu* specialize in smithing and weaving. Outside the artisan subgroups, the Senufo people have hunters, musicians, grave-diggers, diviners, and healers who are called the *Fejembele.* Among these various subgroups, the leatherworkers or *Djelebele* are the ones who have most adopted Islam, although those who convert retain many of their animist practices

Liberia was established by freed American Slaves. The Secret Poro Society there has a connection to the Christian Church. Poro has held people from different villages together. The country was in a civil war for 7 years. Everyone moves out of the Capital to Sierra Leon.

Poro means NEVER DIES. Boys go to Bush School to learn how to survive. Women's Secret Society is Sande or Bunda. They learn to cook and sew, sing and dance. They learn how to be wives and mothers.

The **Baga people** are a **West African** ethnic group who live in the southern swampy lands of **Guinea** Atlantic coastline. Through the pre-colonial times, they were animist, but then they converted to **Islam** during the colonial era. They only converted under the force of Muslim to dominance. Some continue to practice their traditional rituals.

Simo is a Baga Branch of the Poro. The Baga people are independent. They have villages dotted here and there. They don't have a collected state or system. There is no confederation or kingdom. Their population is around 20,000.

Their myth talks about how the world was Marshy or a wet swampy bog. God causes a python to come through the marsh. The python divides the soil from the water. The Python turns into a totem animal. The Baga Python is a symbol for the continuation of life, a sort of rippling motion.

The Baga have the Nimba Mask. Nimba is the Goddess of Fertility. She is a combination of a human woman and a bird. She has a beak like a bird and breasts like a woman. Her ears look like two letter C's on either side of her head. The headdress is often 8 feet tall. Sometimes they will make a miniature version on a dance wand.

The Python Dance includes a Semo Figure that has its hand up to its chin. There is an invisible spout attached to the figure that looks like it is moving. The contents of that funnel, no one knows. Another figure is the Fuhoo, which is a bird woman who lives in the swamp. She taught the Baga how to cultivate rice and use it.

The Baga, unlike other tribes, do not go hungry. They have enough rain. They also raise chicken and goats to eat. The Baga villages specialize in carving as well as weaving, pottery and other things.

April 12, 1996 The Mende and The Dan

The **Mende people** (also spelled **Mendi**) are one of the two largest ethnic groups in Sierra Leone; their neighbors, the Temne people, have roughly the same population. The Mende Tribe also governs by Poro. Women there are a part of Sande and Bandu. Their statue figures are 2 feet tall. Women wear high hair. The Bandu Masks have melon shaped hair. The body is elongated.

Masks are the collective Mind of Mende community. The Collective Mind is viewed as one body; they are the Spirit of the Mende people. The Mende masked figures are a reminder that human beings have a dual existence; they live in the concrete world of flesh and material things and the spirit world of dreams, faith, aspirations and imagination.

The features of a Mende mask convey Mende ideals of female morality and physical beauty. They are unusual because women wear the masks. The bird on top of the head represents a woman's natural intuition that lets her see and know things that others can't. The high or broad forehead represents good luck or the sharp, contemplative mind of the ideal Mende woman. Downcast eyes symbolize a spiritual nature and it is through these small slits that a woman wearing the mask would look out of. The small mouth signifies the ideal woman's quiet and humble character. The markings on the cheeks are representative of the decorative scars girls receive as they step into womanhood. The scars are a symbol of her new, harder life. The neck rolls are an indication of the health of an ideal woman. They have also been called symbols of the pattern of concentric, circular ripples the Mende spirit makes when emerging from the water.

The Nowo dances with the girls and teaches them songs. She carries a whip to create fear and respect. She will also hold their hand during female circumcision. Nowo will lead a funeral procession of a Bandu woman. To the Nowo and the Mende society Black is the most beautiful color. White is the color of eternity though. They weave, sew and make jewelry.

The neck rings at the base of the mask are an exaggeration of actual neck creases. Mende people consider a beautiful neck to be one with rings: they are a sign of beauty because they suggest wealth, high status, and are sexually attractive. The rings indicate prosperity and wholesome living, and are given by God to show his affection for a fortunate few. The rings also indicate a relationship with the divine: the *Sowo* itself is a deity from the waters, and the neck rings represent the concentric waves that are formed on still water by Sowo's head breaking through the surface. The spirit comes from the water, and what the human eye sees on the necks of women "is human in form, but divine in essence", as portrayed in the mask.

The Dan originally came from the western Sudan region to the north, part of present day Mail and Guinea. The location and movements of the Dan, Mano and We can be reconstructed from as early as the 8th century, at which time the Dan and Mano were located in the savanna region of the northern Ivory Coast. In the tenth century, political turmoil, population growth and land depletion caused the Dan to migrate south of the Nimba range and into the high forests.

The Dan are a Mande ethnic group from northwestern Ivory Coast and neighboring Liberia. There are approximately 700,000 members of the group and their largest settlement is Man, Ivory Coast. Neighboring peoples include the Krahn, Kpelle and Mano. They are officially known as Yacouba (or Yakouba) in Ivory Coast. In Liberia, they are also known as Gio. The Dan had a reputation as a fierce warrior society.

The Dan have a complex traditional religion. The Dan believe in Zlan, a Supreme God who created the universe and everything in it. They believe that no one can reach him or see him physically. Instead, they worship *Zu*, an independent spiritual power. The majority of the people believe in reincarnation, through which Zu can enable a person to pass into another person or even an animal after death. The Dan believe that *Zu* is present in all aspects of the universe and is appealed to for many kinds of help. *Zu* is harnessed through masquerade or divination practices; the Dan harness du by creating an object for *du* to embody. Dreaming is the means through which people communicate with *Zu*.

The Poro governs The Dan. They have plain masks for males and females. The plain female masks have slanted or squinted eyes. The nose is spoofed out. There are full lips that are dyed black. There is a white band to keep flies away from the eyes. The male mask has circular eyes with clay around them and no ridge. It has metal teeth.

The terms *ge* and *gle* interchangeably to refer both to Dan masks and to invisible, supernatural spirit forces that live in the forest but esteem to enter the civilized world of the village. The only way they can do this, the **Dan** believe, is through masquerade.

April 15, 1996 Review And Midterm

Review: Dogon and the Tellum as well as the Nummo Twin Myth. The Hogon and Boli Know the Bambara and Senufo. Know about the Baga and Nimba Mask (Goddess of Fertility). Be able to recognize the Dan Masks. The Dan N'Gere Mask keeps away disease. The N'Gere sometimes have warthog tusks or monkey fur. These ugly masks are like gargoyles, keeping away the disfiguring disease or evil.

April 17, 1996 A Return To Laughter

A Return to Laughter is by Elenore Smith Bowen. Laura
Bohannan is her actual name. Bowen is her pen name. Anyway,
Bohannan's undergraduate education was at the **University of
Arizona**, where she met her husband **Paul J. Bohannan**. They
married May 15, 1943. In 1951 Bohannan received her doctorate
from **Oxford University**. Off and on from 1949 to 1953 Bohannan
and her husband lived among the Tiv tribe of southeastern Nigeria.
They would be the subjects of her major works.

Tiv or **Tivi** is an ethno-linguistic group or ethnic nation in West
Africa. The group constitutes approximately 3.5% of Nigeria's total
population, and number about 6.5 million individuals throughout
Nigeria and Cameroon.

A Return To Laughter is a classic of anthropological literature is
a dramatic, revealing account of Anthropologists first year in the
field with a remote African tribe. Simply as a work of ethnographic
interest, *Return to Laughter* Provides deep insights into the culture
of West Africa the subtle web of Tiv tribal life and the power of the
institution of witchcraft. However, the author's fictional approach the
book Tiv gives lasting appeal. She focuses on the human dimension
of anthropology, recounting her Personal Triumphs and failures and
documenting the profound changes she undergoes. As a result, her
story becomes at once universally staff and highly recognizable. She
has brought vividly to life the classic narrative of an outsider caught
up and deeply involved in an utterly alien culture.

Bowen thought she could interact with the tribe, but not quite.
She kept track of the Market Days. She lost three days somehow.
She ended up alone in the bush, which wasn't so good. There were
ants and snakes and other things lurking. Some tribes believe that
heat-lightening witchcraft. The electrical phenomenon of St. Elmo's
Fire is also considered witchcraft.

The main character felt insufficient to help others in the village.
She was able to give them aspirin. Only the strong survive in Africa.
They rarely have access to actual doctors and hospitals. A new baby
was born in the village and the mother named it after the author. No
one told her that the baby died a short time later. The mother had a
lack of emotion over the death of the baby because it was so

common.

Rogo had an important connection to the world. He told the author to stay away from the tribe. He was afraid the tribe could bewitch her. The author chose to go and to write down what she learned. She wanted to believe that people were people no matter where they were from. But the African Culture of the Tiv was vastly different than her own culture. She became depressed when she had trouble connecting with them and trouble understanding their culture.

April 20, 1996 Introduction to Art of the Forest Kingdoms and Baule

The Forrest People or Forest Kingdoms are more concerned with God than the others. Vanity and prestige are important to them. The Kingdoms of Ghana peaked around 1000AD and the Mali peaked at 1325. The Forest Kingdom was swallowed by the Songhai in 1500. The Benin peaked around 1450 and the Kong in 1500.

The **Akan** are a meta-ethnicity predominantly speaking Central Tano languages and residing in the southern regions of the former Gold Coast region where Ghana is located nowadays. Subgroups of the Akan people include:

Asante, Akuapem, **Akwamu**, **Kwahu**, and **Akyem** (together known as Twi), Agona, **Wassa**, **Fante** (Fanti or Mfantse: Anomabo, Abura, Gomua) and **Bono**. Subgroups of the Bia-speaking groups include:**Anyin**, **Baoulé**, Chakosi (Anufo), **Sefwi** (Sehwi), **Nzema**, **A hanta**, and Jwira-Pepesa.

King of Ghana was a deity or his Kingship was divine. The Muslims came in search of slaves around 700 AD. Alibacra wrote this down. The King kept control by taking first-born son of families and trained them to be soldiers. People won't attack the villages with the kingdom soldiers there. He held a huge kingdom like William of Normandy who conquered England. When upper and lower Egypt were united, this created about the same size kingdom as Ghana. Muslims set up libraries and brought both reading and writing to Ghana. The King of Ghana tolerated the Muslims, but it was an uneasy alliance. The Portuguese arrived around 1425.

The People of Ghana believe in Animism and are Matrilineal. While there is a King, they do trace their heritage through Women. Women give the King sons and heirs to the throne. Women even run the court of appeals.

The King is insanely rich with lots of gold. He even has gold dog collars made. The son of a King may have gold plating in his hair. Tradition holds that you can't speak to the King directly. You speak to the Lingual. He will use a long drum and sprinkle dust on the heads of visitors. Visitors must bow. When the Muslim clap, the King must take off his shoes or rather remove his sandals.

The Berbers lived in Algeria. They stirred up a rebellion and the Empire fell. Mansa Moosa lowered the economy of Egypt by handing out gold from Mali. Spanish enrich Judar Rasha went to search for the Gold in 1800 with a Calvary.

The **Songhai Empire** (also transliterated as **Songhay**) was a state that dominated the western Sahel in the 15th and 16th century. At its peak, it was one of the largest states in African history. The state is known by its historiographical name, derived from its leading ethnic group and ruling elite, the Songhai. The Moroccans crushed Songhai. The Moroccans had guns, gun powder and canons. The Songhai retreated south to the Ivory Coast and Ghana. Then they broke into 7 different tribes.

The Serpent of Ouagadougou or For the Soninke people, the decline of their empire was due to the legend of Wagadu, and the rupture of the pact between the empire and the black snake. This happened after the nobles chose Siya Yatabare as the annual sacrifice. She was the most beautiful and "cleanest" virgin girl in that year, but she was also engaged to be married. Her fiancé, Maadi, was the son of Djamere Soukhounou whose unique quality was that he always did what he promised. When Maadi was told him what would happen, that his fiancée would be given to "Bida" - the black snake of Wagadu, he promised Siya that she would not die in the well of Wagadu.

*Siya tried to convince him that it is her destiny, that he should let her to be the gift to the snake in order to save the Empire, but Maadi refused. Within days, he asked his friend, the blacksmith of his village named Bomou, to sharpen his saber. When the day came, Maadi set on his way in the direction of the well of Wagadu. Siya Yatabare was well dressed and her hairstyle was in plaited with gold. The **praise-singer** encouraged her, as did her family. When they left, she saw Maadi and they both fell in tears. Siya told him that if he killed the snake, Wagadu would not have any more rain and the empire would be destroyed forever. Maadi refused, saying* *their destinies are ratified. He left her and hid himself nearby to wait for the snake.*

The snake of Wagadu had seven heads. When the snake took out his first head, Maadi cut it. He did the same to all the others. When the snake took out his last head, the one in silver, the night became clear like the day. The snake said, "I swear by the lord of seven head, during seven years and seven bad years, and during seven months and seven bad months, during seven days and seven bad days, Wagadu will not receive any rain and any piece of gold". Maadi did not mind, and cut the last head. The snake died. Maadi gave to Siya his shoes, the sheath of his saber, his ring, his "danan koufoune" cap. He told her that, if tomorrow they ask you some clarifications, give them those things. Maadi went to his village and told all the details to his mother. She said "you are my only son and it is because of your fiancée that you killed the "Bida", however, the nobles of Wagadu will try to punish you. I swear in the memory of your father that I will do everything to protect you from Wagadu."

*When the sun came up, the nobles asked the praise-singer to go check the well of Wagadu. When they saw Siya, and the heads of the snake in the well, they asked her what happened. As an answer, she gave them the shoes and all the things that Maadi gave her. The nobles of the 99 villages called everybody to come and try to wear the articles of clothing. When Maadi wore the shoes, the bonnet and the ring, everything fit. People knew that he killed the snake. They were going to take him when his mother intervened and said: "I thought there were men in Wagadu, but I do not see any. You are afraid of the prediction of the snake even before you die. But there is something sure, nobody will kill my son because of a snake. I do not see any men here. You will know that my **loincloth** is better than all your trousers accumulated here. During those seven bad years and seven bad months and seven bad days, the needs of Wagadu would be in my charge as an exchange of my son's life and his marriage with Siya Yatabare."*

With shame, the notables of Wagadu concluded the agreement. After Djamere Shoukhouna died, the nobles of Wagadu met and decided that she did what she promised and the agreement was at end and the destiny of the nation would be accomplished. Wagadu went from fertile to dry, and there was no more rain. The children of Dingha, the Soninke, were forced to leave that place which became inhospitable. Thus every family went to his destiny that is the decline of the Ghana Empire - the end of the Soninke Empire.

The Number 7 is key here. It is 7 years, 7 months and 7 Days to cut off 7 Heads. When sand took over and they moved, they split into 7 Tribes.

There is a tribe run by women. There is a Queen Aura Poka. She intermarried with the Senufo and taught them how to carve. The Baule taught the Senufo to do metal work. Nyme is their God. Assye is the Goddess of the Earth. Alura is the Goddess of Creation. The Crocodile is a totem animal. The river could not cross the sacrificial son so the crocodile made a bridge. Hearths were important to them. They used Hot Peppers to keep people from getting infections.

The Statues of the Queen has a rounded body. Sometimes she is sitting, other times she is standing. She is usually found alongside a male statue. He is her other-world mate. Together they represent the ancestral figures Other world mates dressed in contemporary clothes. There is scarification on the statues even though in ancient Ghana there was no scarring or circumcision. Baule has corn rows or rows of braids in her hair, which is the style. The Baule is a spiritual container like a Boli. The use melted wax and gold casting to make it. These spirit containers are worn on a sword and put on a leather sheath.

In 325 AD Monasteries were built in Africa. The Emperor Constantine allowed it seeing as how Christianity was the National Roman Religion at the time. The first Monasteries in Africa were in Egypt and Ethiopia. Monks or teachers made brass crosses.

Circe Purdue is the lost way. It refers to the lost way of **wax casting** also called "investment casting" or "precision casting." It is the process by which a duplicate metal sculpture, which is often **silver, gold, brass** or **bronze** is **cast** from an original sculpture. Intricate works can be achieved by this method. They use tiny wax threads and pile it around a puddle of wet clay. The heavier clay dries and they put it in the fire. They pour sand around it and melt bronze or gold around it. They then throw the clay in the stream and break it. They left with just the cast metal.

April 22, 1996 Baule and Ashanti

Goli is a traditional African dance and masquerade of the Baoulé people of the Ivory Coast. A single performance of a goli last a day. The goli originated among the Wan people, neighbors of the Baoulé.

It was adopted by the Baoulé between 1900 and 1910, perhaps in response to the disruption caused by European colonialism. Today it is the dominant traditional dance form, gradually replacing all others. It may be performed on important occasions, such as funerals, or for entertainment.

The two dancers in a goli wear four different types of traditional masks in a prescribed order: first the disc-shaped kple kple, then the antelope-and-crocodile-inspired goli glen, then the ram-horned kpan pre and finally the human-faced kpan with crested hair. The masks have complex symbolism. In each stage, one mask is "male" and another "female", although the differences between them are subtle, since they represent aspects of one individual. For example, the male kple kple is red and the female is black. The kple kple and the goli glen together constitute the "female" half of the dance, while the later masks are "male". Each mask is also conceived of as having male and female aspects.

They do narrow strip weaving like the Senufo. Used on the traditional narrow-band loom, heddle pulleys are functional objects used to ease the movements of the heddles while separating the warp threads and allowing the shuttle to seamlessly pass through the layers of thread. Like many other carved objects used in everyday activities among the Baule, these pulleys were often embellished for the weaver's delight. Scholars have suggested that the prominent display of pulleys, hanging over the weaver's loom in the public place, afforded artists their best opportunity to showcase their carving skills, in the hope to attract commissions for figures and masks.

The Goli are out alone in the untamed world. They drink Palm wine and eat tripe, which is cow or goat inwards.

The Ashanti are one of the seven tribes that came from Ghana. They are also known as **Asante.** They are an ethnic group that native to the Ashanti Region of modern-day **Ghana**. The Asante speak **Twi.** The language is spoken by over nine million ethnic Asante people as a **first** or second language. Asante is often assumed to mean "because of wars"

They were called as such, because they were always at war with the English who tried to colonize them. A single man held the secular power in the Ashanti Kingdom. The Hene is the leader. English Parliament eventually let the Hene be a part of their parliament and represent the Ashanti Tribe.

The Ashanti believe that if you are sick you go to a mountaintop. You either die on the Mountain or get better and come home. Bodyguards die when the person they are guarding die.

Kente, known as **nwentoma** in Akan, is a type of silk and cotton fabric made of interwoven cloth strips made and native to the Akan ethnic group of Ghana. Kente is made in Akan lands such as the Ashanti Kingdom, They use the narrow strips of cloth that are brightly colored. They weave in specific patterns that are similar to proverbs. It is not that different from the Inca Quipu. Kente cloth is a sign of wealth in their society. The average income is $400 a year and that is how much one Kente cloth costs.

The colors symbolize: black: maturation for intensified spiritual energy, blue for peacefulness, harmony and love, green: vegetation, planting, harvesting, growth, spiritual renewal, gold: royalty, wealth, high status, glory, spiritual purity, gray for healing and cleansing rituals; associated with ash, maroon: the color of mother earth; associated with healing, pink: assoc. with the female essence of life; a mild, gentle aspect of red, purple: assoc. with feminine aspects of life and usually worn by women, red for political and spiritual moods as well as bloodshed or sacrificial rites and death, silver for serenity, purity, joy; associated with the moon, white is purification, sanctification rites and festive occasions, yellow for preciousness, royalty, wealth, fertility, beauty.

Adinkra Cloth are covered in *Adinkra* are **symbols** that represent concepts. *Adinkra* are used extensively in fabrics and pottery among the **Ashantis** of Ashanti Kingdom and the **baoules** who historically migrated from Ghana. *Adinkra* cloths were traditionally only worn by royalty and spiritual leaders for funerals and other very special occasions. In the past they were hand printed on undyed, red, dark brown or black hand-woven cotton fabric depending on the occasion and the wearer's role; nowadays they are frequently mass-produced on brighter colored fabrics If the Hene gives you a Adinkra cloth then you have to be prepared to die for him.

The Amato Symbol are the joined hearts. Akoma means heart.

Ashanti are a matrilineal society where line of descent is traced through the female. Historically, this mother progeny relationship determined **land rights**, inheritance of property, offices and titles. It is also true that the Ashanti inherit property from the paternal side of the family

For 600 years the groups were divided. Then in the 17th Century or 1800s they began to unite under Osei Tutu. Osei Tutu was from a royal family. Menu could not conceive a child, but she got pregnant anyway. Who impregnated her, it was not known. Osei was born to the Menu the Princess. The King took Osei in for 5 years. When he grew up Osei was lustful and handsome. Then he met Anoyke. It was prophesied that Osei Tutu would be the savior of the kingdom. A golden stool fell from the sky as Osei and Anoyke were talking. It was a sign from Yamay that Osei Tutu would be the leader. Osei Tutu became the Ashanti Hene and demanded loyalty. During a national crisis Osei Tutu had to be diplomatic. The Queen of England wanted his stool, which caused a lot of problems. He refused to give it up because it was said to have belonged to the royal family of Ashanti since 1000 BC. It was a reminder that power was in the butt you sat on.

In 1441 the Portuguese first set foot in Accra. Gold was so prevalent that the natives wore a ton of it. They wear a triangle spirit container as well. Art was for prestige for them. It showed authority and money. Stools and carved chairs were important.

The Ashanti have the Kudud vessel that is made of brass or bronze. It represents how the wild is the forest and things are tame in the village. Nuggets are put inside the vessel by the Hene. Villagers put dust in vessel as well. Animals are carved on the box as well as the symbol for infinity. The vessel is buried with you when you die.

Everything is paid for in Gold Dust. The Ashanti are a highly organized society. The Higher the Rank, the Higher your stool. On the 7th Day of the Week they pray to the Ancestral Stool. When you die the stool is blackened and put away. There have been Gold and Silver Stools found in addition to Bronze and Brass.

The Ashanti really don't make masks, but they do make Akwas Ba or *Akua'ba* are wooden ritual fertility **dolls** from **Ghana** and nearby areas. The best-known *akua'ba* are those of the **Ashanti people**, whose *akua'ba* have large, disc-like heads. Other tribes in the region (**Lobi people**) have their own distinctive style of *akua'ba*. Traditionally, these dolls are carried on the back of women either hoping to conceive a child, or to ensure the attractiveness of the child being carried. When not in active use, the *akua'ba* would be ritually washed and cared for.

Jacob Mathew Polkue became the new Ashanti Hene in 1970. He loved spending time in England. RS Rathry is an anthropologist who came in and studied the Ashanti. The study helped decrease tensions and create a better understanding.

April 24, 1996 "A Great Tree Has Fallen" Ashanti and The Yoruba

We watched the short film *"A Great Tree Has Fallen"* about the funeral of the Ashanti Hene Leader. The Tree is Representative of the Ashanti Hene. The sword is a symbol of power. They wear no jewelry when they are mourning. The women wear red. They assign a place for the heads of each tribe for watching the Ashanti Hene's funeral. The ritual is a formalized way of mourning the death of a great leader. There will be a weeklong celebration with music, dances and feasts. On the 6th and 7th Day there will be a cleansing of their things and themselves. There will be the procession of the Golden Stool and the final feast is on the 7th Day. The new Ashanti Hene will sit on the Golden Stool.

The **Yorùbá people** (also: **Ioruba** or **Joruba)** are an African ethnic group that inhabits western Africa. The Yoruba constitute about 105 million people in total. The majority of this population is from Nigeria, where the Yorùbá make up 21% of the country's population.

The Yoruba have evolved a complicated cosmology. According to the Yoruba creation myth, during a certain stage in this process, the "truth" was sent to confirm the habitability of the newly formed planets. The **earth** being one of these was visited but deemed too wet for conventional life. All human beings possess what is known as *"Ayanmo"* or destiny and fate. They are expected to eventually become one in spirit with Olodumare because Olorun is the divine creator and source of all energy. The thoughts and actions of each person in *Ayé,* or the he physical realm, interact with all other living things, including the Earth itself. Each person attempts to achieve transcendence and find their destiny in Orun-Rere, the spiritual realm of those who do good and beneficial things.

The Yoruba believe the world is square. The hierarchy is Olorun, Odudwa, Oni of Ife, the 16 Obas and then Major and Minor Chiefs. Finally, the heads of family is at the bottom of the hierarchy.

April 29, 199 7 Yoruba and Benin City

The **Nok culture** is an early **Iron Age** population whose material remains are named after the **Ham** village of **Nok** in **Kaduna State** of **Nigeria**, where their famous **terracotta** sculptures were first discovered in 1928. The Nok Culture appeared in **northern Nigeria** around 1500 BC and vanished under unknown circumstances around 500 AD, thus having lasted approximately 2,000 years.

All we have are heads from their life size statues. The Nok are probably the ancient Yoruba. The eyes on the statues are unique. The eye lids are heavy and purple lips that dips downward. The nostrils are as wide as the corners of the mouth. The Nok heads have pierced mouths. There are also Nok Elephant Heads with long narrow faces. The Nok heads were Alter Pieces associated with the Yoruba Creations Myth.

The Palace of Ooni of Ife: According to the traditions of the Yoruba, Ife was founded by the order of the Supreme God Olodumare by **Obatala**. It then fell into the hands of his sibling **Oduduwa**, which created enmity between the two. Oduduwa created a dynasty there, and sons and daughters of this dynasty became rulers of many other kingdoms in Yoruba-land.

The first Oòni of Ife is a descendant of Oduduwa, which was the 401st Orisha. The present ruler since 2015 is Oba Adeyeye Enitan Ogunwusi Ojaja II. Ooni of Ife who is also an Accountant from Nigeria. Named as the city of 401 deities, Ife is home to many worshipers of these deities and is where they are routinely celebrated through festivals. Ilé-Ifè is famous worldwide for its ancient and naturalistic bronze, stone and terracotta sculptures, dating back to between 1200 and 1400 A.D.

The Ooni of Ife reign is for 7 days or years. The people killed him by bashing his head in. He can't get ill and isn't allowed to age. He has to be murdered in his prime. When the Ooni of Ife dies a bronze head his made. It is a hollow head with a crown. There is a beard attached to the head and clothes are put on a wooden body. A puppet head is in place and paraded around. The body is burned.

The Tada figure is found in the Jada Village. The Tada is an Alter Figure. It is a Nok figure in a sitting position. The British couldn't find the Tada figure because it was buried. The Nok would rub sand on it as they prayed so much so that they arms and legs would be rubbed off of the statute.

Ife was like a mecca for ancient Yoruba. Like in the novel *Things Fall Apart,* people would come to see the Oracle. There is a bird on the staff.

Oshan is the Venus of the Yoruba. She has typical hair and is holding her breasts. Eshu is the God of Enforcement. He is both like the police and the trickster. Eshu partially serves as an alternate name for Eleggua, the messenger for all Orishas, and that there are 256 paths to Eleggua—each one of which is an Eshu. It is believed that Eshu is an Orisha similar to Eleggua, but there are only 101 paths to Eshu according to ocha, rather than the 256 paths to Eleggua according to Ifá. Eshu is known as the "Father who gave birth to Ogboni", and is also thought to be agile and always willing to rise to a challenge

If the Trickster finds you and you are not doing things right, then he will have a tree fall you or a car hit you. You have to pray to Eshu before you pray to Alron. The top of the Eshu masks have hair shaped like penis on it. He often has buck teeth or bunny teeth. If you are lazy or aroused and don't do your work you can claim Eshu made you do it.

From 1967 to 1969 was a Civil War fought over the idea of twins. The Ebo and Yoruba clashed over their beliefs. Ebo was landlocked. The US took their side. Russia took Ebo's side. They starved the Ebo. The Ebo believed that twins were not a soul mate or twin flame or soul sister/brother. They Ebo believed twins were evil. The Yoruba believed that twins shared the same soul.

Yoruba peoples have one of the highest incidents of twin births in the world. As a result, twins are regarded as extraordinary beings protected by Sango, the deity of thunder. They are believed to be capable of bestowing immense wealth upon their families or misfortune to those who do not honor them. Powerful spirits in life, twins are honored with carved memorial figures when they die. These figures, known as *ere ibeji* (literally meaning *ere*: sacred image; *ibi*: born; *eji*: two), remain a point of access to the spirit of the departed individual. The mother provides ritual care to the figures, bathing, dressing, adorning, and feeding them. Such daily handling is responsible for giving their surface its distinctive patina. *Ere ibeji* invariably represent their subjects with mature adult physiognomies, and are often crowned with elaborate hairdos.

The Yoruba are famous for their divination practices. The use a bowl with flour and a cola nut. The pattern of the nuts in the flour is red and the future is told. There are sixteen major books in the Odu Ifá literary corpus. When combined, there are a total of 256 Odu that are believed to reference all situations, circumstances, actions and consequences in life based on the uncountable ese (or "poetic tutorials") relative to the 256 Odu coding. These form the basis of traditional Yoruba spiritual knowledge and are the foundation of all Yoruba divination systems. Ifá proverbs, stories, and poetry are not written down. Rather, they are passed down orally from one *babalawo* to another

The Gelede mask is more accurately a headdress, since it rests on top of the wearer's head and a cloth veil covers face. The headdress takes the form of a human head, on top of which are motifs that are intended to entertain onlookers but, in addition, usually address social concerns that may also be expressed in songs that are part of the masquerade. The headdresses are usually brightly painted.

The **Gẹlẹdẹ** spectacle of the Yoruba is a public display by colorful masks, which combines art and ritual dance to amuse, educate and inspire worship. Gelede celebrates "Mothers" (*awon iya wa*), a group that includes female ancestors and deities as well as the elderly women of the community, and the power and spiritual capacity these women have in society. However, this power may also be destructive and take the form of witchcraft; therefore, Gelede serves the function of appeasing this power, as well

This vibrantly colored Janus-faced mask reflects the diversity of Egungun masks of the Yoruba. *Egungun* means masquerade, and these masks are used in Odun Egungun festivals, which are performed for ancestors throughout the Yoruba region. This mask's elaborately grooved horns and central conical coiffure, which is painted blue, rise dramatically from the mask's two faces. Two monkey figures once ran down the horns with front legs perched on the head, but one of the monkeys is now missing. The horns may signify its use as a hunter's mask. Hunters are one of the few Yoruba social groups that are linked across different lineages and who have their own Egungun masqueraders.

Shango (Ṣàngó) is an Orisha. Genealogically speaking, Shango is a royal ancestor of the **Yoruba** as he was the third Alaafin of the **Oyo Kingdom** prior to his posthumous deification. He is considered to be one of the most powerful rulers that Yorubaland has ever produced, and is noted for his anger. He had many wives and children. He was a cruel man, so Aloron punished him. He was sorry for his errors and so his wealth was restored. Shango carries a double-headed ax.

Drums, called *Agba,* were considered sacred objects. A round, single-headed standing drum on four short legs, made of hard, heavy wood. The resonance body is under the pegs of the leather drum. On the front side of the drum a relief with an abstract depiction of the earth goddess 'Onile'. They received sacrificial offerings and were used only for ritual ceremonies. The present *Agba drum* was originally colored red and white.

May 1, 1996 "*The Kingdom of Bronze*"

The Tribal Eye TV Series, Episode **Kingdom of Bronze** (1975) At the turn of the century Europeans refused to believe that the craftsmen of the Nigerian Kingdom of Benin could have made such sophisticated and beautiful bronze castings. This program traces the history of Beni and Yoruba bronzes, and examines the techniques used in making them, and the results. We see the beautiful and elegant portrait busts, plaques and standing figures which read as impressive chronicles of the elaborate court life under the autocratic Obas of Benin.

Benin City was the principal city of the Edo kingdom of Benin, which flourished during the 13th to the 19th century. It was destroyed in 1897 by the British after the Edo assaulted an earlier British expedition, which had been told not to enter the city during a religious festival but nonetheless attempted to do so. Both Europeans and Africans were killed. Only two Europeans survived. They got word back to London and the English attacked Benin City. Before burning the city down, the British pillaged it, taking many of its famous bronzes, ivory, and other treasures

The Benin are NOT the Yoruba. The Benin City is where the Benin Tribe Live. The Queen Mother heals with Magic and Medicine. Only by blood can the land be purified. The Climax of the Festival is Human Sacrifice. The Igue-isha was transported from the Ife. They created the Palm Oil that is in Palmolive Dish Soap.

Igue festival is a celebration with its origin in the Benin Kingdom. It was originally celebrated as a festival to renew Oba **Ewuare**'s magical powers. One tradition states that the festival date coincided with the marriage of Ewuare to a wife named Ewere. Celebrated between Christmas and New Year, the festival includes the Oba's blessing of the land and his people. During the Igue ritual season, the Oba is prohibited from being in the presence of any non-native person.

The Oba died in 1913, His son rules today. Servants and Assistants surround him. A dwarf looks after the shrines. The palace is always filled with singing and music. When they announce that Oba is in the palace, the doors open. There is a sacred shrine that belongs to Oba. There is a Bell Spirit of the Ancestors. The Bell Represents prayer.

The Queens all have distinct hair styles The Oba once had over 100 wives. He oversaw all of them being raised, except one who was sent away. Women all have to make sacrifices.

Bronze Casting was introduced to the people of Benin City. The Benin people owned structures and wanted to be part of the Yoruba people. The Oba received a petal shaped sword. The Benin could not rule unless the Oòni of Ife received the sword. The ruler was buried at Ife. Inside the tomb were two figures cast in bronze.

There were 11 men's heads casts in copper. There was an elephant tooth as well. Ivory was the first thing carved by the Benin. The darker the ivory, the older it is. The Benin created compact, rounded figures with fleshy cheeks and coral necklaces. The alter pieces have black feet.

In Benin City people walked into court naked so they could not carry concealed weapons. In the Year 1280 Oba asked Ooni of Ifa for a Bronze Caster. Oranmyan the son of Oduduwa went to Benin City. He married the daughter of a local chief. He gave his son the throne and left. Igue-isha had a bronze castor. Now the necks of the Benin have metal coil necklaces and coral necklaces. The flesh of their eyes are pushed up as well.

The Queen Mother's head was cast on bronze. Bronze was used for their pectoral pendants and for their Petal Shaped swords. They made cuffs of Ivory. The Benin wear tattoos. They also play the flute at beheadings.

Oba turned Christian in later years, although he hung onto the Animism elements of his religion. Plaques were made in Bronze to cover pillars. Some plagues have history lessons carved on them. Oba had to Leopards as bodyguards. Ivory Leopards were carved to celebrate. Oba also kept an elephant tusk from a warrior who had killed the

The Play *Trapped* by Benin Villager: There are three characters and a narrator. There is Ama the mother and Emiko the father. Oda is the son. His Christian name is Paul. It is a rainy night and he is having nightmares. Is there a bad omen? Is the husband just paranoid? If they are Christians they shouldn't worry about sacrifices and destiny, but they do. His parents want to go back to the rituals. Well, his father does. His mother doesn't.

There is hatred between the religions divisions. They feel alienated. The children are being taught Britain's History. The father feels like they are losing their culture and their respect. The son is into British things and not his home Africa. The son is going to England. The mother will leave if her son goes to England. The Father is upset with his son's rebellion. The Father's word was law. Now it isn't.

The tragedy is that the father didn't consider change before rejecting it and the son didn't think about his change before accepting it. The father clings to the old ways because it is the only thing he has ever known. The father is sad at the loss of his culture and his family. He tells them they will be accepted if they fail and come back.

May 6, 1996 Things Fall Apart and Ebo

Ebo is not a Kingdom. It is a loose confederation of tribes. The **Igbo people** also spelled **Ibo** and formerly also *Iboe, Ebo, Eboe, Eboans, Heebo or Ṇ́dị̀ Ìgbò* are an ethnic group native to the present-day south-central and southeastern Nigeria. There has been much speculation about the origins of the Igbo people, as it is unknown how exactly the group came to form. Geographically, the Igbo homeland is divided into two unequal sections by the Niger River – an eastern (which is the larger of the two) and a western section. The Igbo people are one of the largest ethnic groups in Africa.

Bantu is what the Ebo speak. They also make the Mmwo Mask. It represents Female Ghosts, especially mothers. *Agbogho mmwo,* or "maiden spirit," masks are worn by men at festivals that honor important deities. They represent the Igbo ideal of female beauty: small, balanced features, elaborate hairstyles, and delicate tattoos. The men who dance *agbogho mmwo* masks wear colorful, tight-fitting fiber costumes, entertaining the crowd with exaggerated versions of women's dances.

There is also the Maji mask with sharp, chiseled features. These are brightly colored masks that are cubist in nature. It is flat plane against flat plane. They use these for harvest festivals.

Ikenga (Igbo literal meaning "strength of movement") is a **horned Alusi** found among the Igbo people in southeastern Nigeria. It is one of the most powerful symbols of the Igbo people and the most common cultural artifact. Ikenga is mostly maintained, kept or owned by men and occasionally by women of high reputation and integrity in the society. It comprises someone's *Chi* (personal god), his Ndichie (Ancestor's) aka *Ikenga* (right hand), *ike* (power) as well as spiritual activation through prayer and sacrifice. It is often a figure of a man standing holding a plate. The power is in the right arm.

Perhaps the most popular and renowned novel that deals with the Igbo and their traditional life was the 1959 book by Chinua Achebe, ***Things Fall Apart***. The novel concerns influences of British colonialism and Christian missionaries on a traditional Igbo community during an unspecified time in the late nineteenth or early 20th century. Most of the novel is set in Umuofia, one of nine villages on the lower Niger.

The Ebo are more into God. Chi is the personal God. Chuck Woo is another name for God. Chinua Achebe and his brother Benjamin lived with their teacher. He taught them that the artist is separate from politics. Each person has a single soul that does die. The Ebo's concept is that the soul is Eternal. Humans, Plants and Animals all have souls. The Soul goes to God when we die. In rare cases, an evil Spirit will take the soul.

There is a medicine house or a shrine that they keep. In Ebo-land there is no funeral for a person after they die. It is tradition to wait three or four years before a funeral is held. If a funeral is never held than a person's spirit will haunt old houses and burial grounds. The souls of those who commit suicide or were thrown into the bush or a river will come back as an animal.

There was a sacrifice before the war. A girl replaces the wife who died. Ikemfuna was the sacrifice Okonkun is a great wrestler and his father lazy. He died of a disfiguring disease. That means he can't have a funeral or be buried properly. He drank Palm wine from the head of an enemy and was a great warrior, so it is tragic he can't have a funeral.

Okonkwo shows no affection only anger and then he was killed. He had a hand in the boy's death and ended up dead because of it.

May 8, 1996 Sao, Cameroon Grasslands

The **Sao civilization** flourished in Central Africa from the Cameroon Grasslands. the sixth century BC to as late as the sixteenth century AD. The Sao lived by the Chari River Around Lake Chad in territory that later became part of Cameroon and **Chad**. They are the earliest people to have left clear traces of their presence in the territory of modern Cameroon. Sometime around the 16th century, conversion to Islam changed the cultural identity of the former Sao.

The movie *The African Queen* had the backdrop of the Cameroon Grasslands. The 1951 film stars Humphrey Bogart and Katherine Hepburn. There is a German boat on Lake Chad and the two of them sink the German boat and fall in love during WWII.

Anyway, the Sao art is unusual. They are known for their terracotta anthropomorphic statuettes which are up to 35 cm high and appear with numerous scarifications and rough features. Some were excavated from sanctuaries, while others were found in burial sites. Pierced zoomorphic figures are thought to have been used either as currency or as ritual objects. The Sao also made bronze jewelry – bronze bracelets and pendants were often decorated around the edges with an undulated motif.

The Cameroon Grasslands are a narrow ridge of land between the countries of Nigeria and Chad. In 1884 Germans arrived. In 1886 a plantation system was implemented. It is the only place in Africa where there are plantations with African Slaves. In the 1900s it became a famous place.

The Bantu who live in Cameroon Grasslands are a Matrilineal Society. King Njoya of Bamum came in and he changed things to Patrilineal.

They have stylized headpieces with puffy cheeks and ears that stick out. The masks have an open mouth that is almost smiling. There are spider legs carved on the top like a crown. If it isn't a spider, it is some other creature. One mask had snakes carved on top of it. There are no eye holes. The mask is worn at a slant so the wearer can see downward.

The Highest ranking member of their society wears a cap made of human hair. One figure they found was nearly 3D. There are statues with crisscross threads and beads. They use fabric to sew designs onto the wood.

There is art in everyone's home in the Cameroon. There are lots of beaded work. They also did a lot of Bronze casting. One item has a Scepter Top. It is associated with the Dog Cult. There is also an Elephant Society that wears a mask with eye holes and beads. One of these Elephant Masks was featured in a McDonald's commercial recently!

You have to have a stool with a monkey holding it up. Those are famous. There are also Buffalo or Bush Cow Figures or Masks. Strips of cloth and beads cover those figures as well.

They have a ridgepole figure with human hair that hold Palm Wine and smoking pipes. Most of the Bantu smoke and drink every day. A man of great status will have one on his roof. The men of the grasslands wear loin clothes only or at least they did. Now most of them wear traditional Muslim clothing.

The Style of Architecture is carved pillars, large thatched roofs. They have square houses with round roofs and grass floors. Everything is carved. Fashion: Women wear big earrings. Their hair grows in tufts. They often wear cam wood in their hair. They practice scarification.

May 13, 1996 Fang, (Ba) Kohta and African Art of 20th Century

The **Fang people**, also known as **Fãn** or **Pahouin**, are a Central African ethnic group found in Equatorial Guinea, northern **Gabon**, and southern Cameroon. Nzami is the God. He reserved the Heaven for himself. The Elephant represents wisdom. The Leopard is a symbol of all that is strong an fast. The Monkey represents Malice.

The First Man was wicked and arrogant. He didn't want to worship God. He wanted everyone for himself. Trees dried up and burnt down. Everything died. The first man was burned alive. Eventually the trees grew again. Now when one digs up the earth they find the hard black rock that still burns. This is coal, but they see it as the remains of the first man and the old forest.

The Second Man is the father of all humans called Sacumie and women came from a tree Ombomay. Nasisim causes shadows. Nasisim lives in the eye. He is the soul. They believe the body dies, but the soul does not.

Reliquary Guardian are figures that guard the head of dead. Reliquary is box of possession the Catholic Church with items from various Saints. The Fang have a similar box. The Fang also have hats with beads. Behind the eyes of they have tar or pitch. The figures have full and rounded shapes. The heads look like skulls with metal around the eyes. The figure holds a yam and a cutting knife. It is given an overall black shiny look.

The Fang have several secret societies. Their dance masks are almost like the Baule and their two dimensional masks. Picasso and his roommate love these masks and thus began Cubism.

The **Bakota** (or Kota) are a Bantu **ethnic group** from the north-eastern region of Gabon. The language they speak is called **iKota**, but is sometimes referred to as Bakota, Ikuta, Kota, and along the Fang, they are known as Mekora. he Kota are traditionally a **patriarchal** society, however some of   the sub-groups such as the Mahongwe have over time adopted a matrilineal system of lineage.

They are noted for their copper and **brass** reliquary guardian figures, which are part of a powerful religious and mystical order known as **Bwete**. Another key feature of the Kota people is the originality of its circumcision and widow-purification rituals, which are generally kept secret.

The Bakota have reliquary guardians as well. It is always a big head with bent knees. The Crescent goes left to right on male but up and down on women. These particular sculptures inspired Picasso. He felt he had discovered a 4th Dimension. Picasso turned African art every which way for his pieces.

The Bakota have scarification masks. Sometimes shiny metal paper will be placed over the masks. Once in a while the masks will have closed eyes.

CUBISM is analytic and synthetic. It is different from Leonardo Di Vinci's realistic looking Art. The camera was in use in 1909. This changed the need for realistic looking art. Art didn't have to reflect the real world. It could be anything.

Picasso's *Les Demoiselles d'Avignon* marks a radical break from traditional composition and perspective in painting. It depicts five naked women with figures composed of flat, splintered planes and faces inspired by Iberian sculpture and African masks. The compressed space the figures inhabit appears to project forward in jagged shards; a fiercely pointed slice of melon in the still life of fruit at the bottom of the composition teeters on an impossibly upturned tabletop.

African Art was considered dirty or pornographic before, but

Picasso saw it for its beauty and took inspiration from it. Picasso was born in Spain and taught to paint realistically. He also picked up Paul Cezanne's style of flattening things. Cezanne didn't try to pull people in. He just used splashes of color.

Paul Gauguin was born in Brazil. He joined the Coast Guard. He became familiar with the South Pacific. He ended up in Scandinavia. He married in Denmark and then went to Paris. He did well as a stock broker and was wealthy. He had five children. He started painting with them. He used egg to temper the oil paints. He went broke when he focused on painting. He took his wife and children back to Denmark.

Gauguin painted with Van Gogh in the South of France. They used very thick paint with lead in it. Van Gogh got lead poisoning. Due to the lead poisoning he grew angry and cut off his ear and sent it to a prostitute. Gauguin got fed up with behavior and left Van Gogh for Tahiti. He married a 13 year old . There he painted in the flat, horizontal style.

In 1901 Picasso painted physical disabilities. He painted a blind guitarist and woman suffering from pain as she ironed. Picasso used blue during his "*Blue Period.*" Picasso also drank. He also got art from Sailors. He asked them to bring him pieces from thier travels. Tarzan and other works of literature romanticized the noble savages of Africa. This was an influence as well.

In 1907 Picasso was paid to paint at the World's Fair. He did allegorical paintings. He cautioned young men against using houses of prostitution and getting STDs. There would always be fruit in the background as a symbol of sensuality. He also made them have exaggerated gestures. He often added African Masks to the background of his paintings. He also sculpted the Mistress from Baga Nimba Mask.

Analytical Cubism consists of browns, grays, tans and greens. They keep to Earth Colors. They cut the space into squares. The portraits are then distorted. Synthetic Cubism is the addition of papers or cloth. It is like a collage. The colors can also include red, among others. There will be an overlapping and transfusing of shapes. The painter will look at the portrait from different viewpoints and include them all.

Amedeo Clemente Modigliani (July 1884 – 1920) was an **Italian** Jewish **painter** and **sculptor** who worked mainly in France. He is known for portraits and nudes in a **modern** style characterized by elongation of faces, necks, and figures that were not received well during his lifetime but later found acceptance. Modigliani spent his youth in Italy, where he studied the art of antiquity and the Renaissance. In 1906 he moved to Paris, where he came into contact with such artists as Pablo Picasso and Constantin Brâncuşi. By 1912 Modigliani was exhibiting highly stylized sculptures with Cubists of the Section d'Or group at the Salon d'Automne.

Mary 15, 1996 Mary Kingsley and The Bakongo

The scientific studies of Mary Kingsley (1862-1900) added much to European knowledge of African wild-life. She brought back one previously unknown species of fish, six new subspecies that had not been named, a previously unknown snake, and eight new insects. It was a great achievement for someone with no scientific training.

Kingsley boated down the river between two nations. The small river they went down was not on a map. One of the kingdoms was friendly and the other bad. In the village of Mofeta, they picked up a guy named "Duke." Their guide would stop every two hours so he could rest, smoke and eat. On one of the rests they discovered human remains. The traveled from the good village to the evil village. They traveled through a mangrove swamp.

When Kingsley finally met the Fang, they ran down from their village with weapons, clearly intending to attack her and the men in the canoe. She and the men stood still, holding out their hands. Luckily, one of the Fang men recognized one of the men in Kingsley's boat: they had traded with each other before. Kingsley asked for men to accompany her deeper into the interior, and eventually reached an agreement. Through their travels together, Kingsley and the Fang developed a sense of mutual respect

According to Desmond Wilcox in the novel **Ten Who Dared,** she wrote, "There is something reasonable about trade, especially if you show yourself an intelligent trader who knows the price of things. It enables you to sit as an honored guest at far-away inland village fires: it enables you to become the confidential friend of that ever-powerful factor in all human societies, the old ladies. It enables you to become an associate of the confraternity of Witch Doctors, things that being surrounded with an expedition of armed men must prevent you're doing." George Kingsley, Mary's Uncle, wrote the book.

There was a movie made of the book in the 1970s

The **Bakongo** are also known as The Kongo. Ba means people of the Bantu Migration. The origin of the name Kongo is unclear, but according to scholar Samuel Nelson, the term *Kongo* is possibly derived from a local verb for gathering or assembly. The originated near Ebo. They worked metal and had a wide loom system of weaving.

As they migrated inland, they absorbed other tribes, bringing farming with them. By the 15th Century they had large kingdoms. The symbol for the Kongo tribes was a woman nursing a child. In the Kongo the slave trade thrived. The Christians, who drove out the Moors or the Muslims, used the bible and idea that Noah's son Ham was the one who spawned the Africans.

The Portuguese led the era of discovery. They viewed Henry as saving the world. The Portuguese fought in Morocco. Prince Henry set up a school of Navigation with Map Makers, Astronomers, Sailors and Ship Builders. Europe was not interested in Africa until after that. Until 1518 Portugal was the only one colonizing.

Blacks came to Portugal and got baptized. They went back to Africa to teach their fellow men what they learned in Europe. In 1460 some 500 slaves were transported to Brazil. Later that number grew to 670 per year. In 1518 Slaves were sent directly to to the New World.

Because of the Explorers new food and plants were introduced from both Europe and the New World. Maize or Corn, Tobacco, Tomatoes and Citrus Fruits. Sweet Potatoes and Pineapples were brought from Africa to the New World as well.

The Congo River is the base of many tribes. In 1845 **Mvemba a Nzinga** or **Nzinga Mbemba** (c. 1456–1542 or 1543), also known as **King Afonso I**, was a ruler of the Kingdom of Kongo in the first half of the 16th century. He reigned over the Kongo Empire from 1509 to late 1542 or 1543. He was baptized Christian. Faith had diminished in the area with the slave trade.

The People of the Congo were the first Modern Christians in Africa. They set up trade and embarrassed the Western World. In 1538 the Portuguese gave up in Benin. In 1657 the Missionaries came back and were expelled. See the movie *Kingdom of Bronze.* 1526 Alfonzo made an appeal to the King of Portugal. He said send me two doctors and two pharmacists as well as priests and teachers. We could also use wine and flour. The Portuguese did not respond.

By 1700 there was no evidence of Western Education or Western Life in the Congo. Slavery was better for those in exile than dying alone in the wilderness. Tribes would sell prisoners of war into slavery. There was the attitude that other tribes were inferior to your tribe in Africa. The Slave Trade took its toll. Millions of African had been sold to Europe and the New World by the Mid-1800s.

It is important to know two particular forms of Art from the Congo or Bakongo. There is the Maternity Figure and the Alter Piece. Notice there is no scarification markings on the Fang Art. But on the Bakongo there is scarring on the shoulders of the women figures. There are necklaces across the breast and a simple hair do. One figure has a beaded cap, broad shoulders and thing legs. Another is playing a drum while holding a baby. Christians didn't destroy the figures because they reminded the Christians of the Virgin Mary and Jesus figures in their own religion.

Fetish in Portuguese means "hollow." It is a hollow figure with a plug in its belly. The Fetish may contain potions or poisons. The Voodoo Dolls that came to the Caribbean were based off of Fetish Figures. Fetish's original use was to keep harmony. It wasn't to curse. A Mirror Fetish has a mirror in the figure's belly instead of a plug. The Mirror is used to swear on. A person would have to put their tongue on the mirror and then swear they didn't do something. If you lie the Fetish would make you get sick. The whole village would use the Fetish. It wasn't for Private Use. There is also the Nail Fetish. You drive a Nail into a body and swear that you didn't do it. If you lied, you get sick. There are also Animal Fetishes. You must have committed a terrible crime to demand to use the Fetish.

May 20, 1996 Bakuba and Baluba

The Bakuba are of Zaire. The **Kuba Kingdom**, also known as the **Kingdom of the Bakuba** or **Bushongo**, is a Kingdom in Central Africa. The Kuba Kingdom **flourished** between the 17th and 19th centuries in the region bordered by the **Sankuru, Lulua**, and Kasai rivers in the south-east of the modern-day Democratic Republic of the Congo.

The leader is considered divine. He is a warrior who preaches peace and love toward enemies. There is a picture of the Shambo who ruled in in 1971. Europe introduced metal needles for sewing and metal nails for building, which was very important to them.

Note the elegant cloth and heavy costume. The cloth is woven with brass thread and lots of cowrie shells. The more shells, the wealthier the person. If you are an important person you will receive a cowrie shell belt.

The men weavers have 12 inches of loom to use. Women's cloth design is stenciled on. The use natural colors such as brown, black and gold. Sometimes they use purple. The Kuba are known for their raffia embroidered textiles, fiber and beaded hats, carved palm wine cups and cosmetic boxes, but they are most famous for their monumental helmet masks, featuring exquisite geometric patterns, stunning fabrics, seeds, beads and shells. They have been described as a people who cannot bear to leave a surface without ornament.

The Royal Portrait Figure or the Shamba Bolongongo. The figure is made of wood and has a flat crown. It is 18 to 24 inches tall and looks fleshy. It has heavy features. The heaviness represents its power. Each statue is different because it commemorates a different leader or Shamba.

The back of figures show evidence of scarification. Bakuba also make cosmetic boxes. These boxes serve as grave markers. They also made a series of Palm Wine drinking cuts in the shape of human and animals heads. No Bakuba travels without Palm Wine!

The Kuba believed in Bumba the Sky Father who spewed out the sun, moon, stars, and planets. He also created life with the Earth Mother. However these were somewhat distant deities, and the Kuba placed more immediate concern in a supernatural being named Woot, who named the animals and other things. Woot was the first human and bringer of civilization. The Kuba are sometimes known as the "Children of Woot."

Zaire was a Belgium Colony, but the Belgian left. The King of Zaire in 1996 declared himself God and bled his people dry. Zaire is a very corrupt place now.

The Baluba developed a society and culture by about the 400s CE, later developing a well-organized community in the Upemba Depression known as the Baluba confederation. Luba society consisted of miners, smiths, woodworkers, potters, crafters, and people of various other professions. Their success and wealth grew greatly over time, but this also caused their gradual decline to marauding bands of slavers, robbers, and terrorists from among Portuguese and Omani led influenced invasions.

The Kabila Figure is the Daughter of Spirit. It is a bowl that is carved by pregnant women who can't work. People give her food. They put food in her bowl with a statue.

The Traditional Bali is round, with quiet features. They have long style faces, eyes that are sunken. They have thin lines for eyebrows. They have sharp, angular limbs and tubular limbs. There is a cross in the back with the hairstyles. Scarification is elaborate around the Bellybutton. They often have long waterfall like hairstyles. The women have a special neck rest to preserve their wonderful hairdos

They have a spoon with a human head or face carved on the top of the handle. They also have Traditional Caryatid Figures. The Figure is on its knees, which is a position of respect. The stool has a figure holding it up. It is almost like balloons holding it up.

Of the several mask types used by the Luba, one of the better known is *kifwebe*, a mask elaborated with whitened parallel grooves on a dark ground. The *kifwebe* masks, used by the secret society of the same name, originated in this territory. The Luba attribute its origins to three spirits, which emerged from a ditch near a lake. The female spirit was attracted by humans and went to live among them. The two male spirits stayed in the bush, but visited the village where they dazzled the inhabitants with their dancing to the point where the men begged to be initiated. These distinctive masks vary a great deal but in general are characterized by lineal patterns all over the face.

The traditional Baluba Mask is round with no grooves. There are eyes, but they are closed. Bulls or rams horns are often attached. They use them for rites of passage.

The Baluba have listen and response music. It is pleasant music and not aggressive. There are drums. It is more choir like. In *Things Fall Apart* the son is drawn to the church of the Christians by the upbeat music

The appellation *Hamitic* was applied to the **Berber, Cushitic**, and **Egyptian** branches of the Afroasiatic language family. People are influenced by these Hamites in the North Eastern Corner of Zaire. They are physically different from the Bakuba.

May 22, 1996 Review

We viewed Slides. Ibo Dead Mother and Son Cutting Yams Figures, Sao Terracotta Figures and Cameroon Grasslands figures. Slides of Fang Reliquary Guardian with the oozing tar. Slide of the masks that influenced Picasso. Slides of Bakota and Bakongo. Ba means people of. Bakongo Maternal figure that reminded Missionaries of Virgin Mary. Slides of the VERY Decorative Bakuba figures and Shamba cloths. Focus heavily on Bakuba and Baluba boxes, weapons and masks.

May 27, 1996 Memorial Day
May 29, 1996 African Meal and Projects Room 117 in Bromfield

Cooking Journal

April 29, 1996: I talked with Mrs. Alemendinger about my project. I asked her where I could find some recipes. I had meant to get started earlier, but I had put it off. She told me any library book would do and to look specifically at either African or International Cookbooks.

May 3, 1996: I finally found the time to go to the Mansfield Library. I picked out one African Cookbook and one International Cookbook.

May 5, 1996: After a busy weekend, I sat down to look at the books I got. Most the recipes called for chicken, fish or lamb. I couldn't afford to fix anything too expensive, since I don't have a job right now. Thankfully, Mom agreed to pay for some ingredients. In addition, a lot of recipes called for hot peppers, which I am not too fond of. I decided to try Banana Fritters and Pineapple Thirst Quencher.

May 18, 1996: Because I don't have a car and it was nearly impossible to get to the store, I had to set up a time to go with Mom. I wrote down what I needed. Some of the stuff I already had at home. This is what I bought: *Granulated Sugar $1.79, Flour 79 Cents, Pineapple Chunks 99 Cents, Milk 49 Cents, Bananas $1.34, Oranges $2.59.* All together it came to $6.70. Some of the things I compromised on. Instead of a whole pineapple, I bought chunks and instead of skimmed, I got 2 Percent Milk. I didn't realize until I got home that I needed the pineapple peel as well as the chunks, so I probably should have bought the whole pineapple. Oops. You Live, Your Learn. I don't cook very much, so this all new to me.

Banana Fritters

Makes 2 Servings of 6 Fritters Each for a Total of 12 Fritters. The Recipe is from West Africa.
1 Medium Banana, peeled and cut into pieces.
1/2 Cup of Skim Milk
1 Egg
1/2 Teaspoon of Vanilla Extract
1 1/3 Cup of All Purpose Flour
1 1/2 Teaspoons of Granulated Sugar
2 Teaspoons of Vegetable Oil, divided
1 Teaspoon of Confectioners' Sugar
In a blender container combine banana, milk, eggs and vanilla and process until pureed, scraping down the sides of the container as necessary. Add flour and sugar and process, stopping motor the motor to scrape sides down. Pour into bowl and let stand for 30 Minutes. In a 12 inch nonstick skillet heat 1 teaspoon of oil over high heat and stir batter, about half of it. Drop mixture in by teaspoon fulls into skillet and brown the bottom. Cook until bubbles appear on surface and then flip. Use remaining teaspoon of oil and batter and repair until six fritters have been made. Sprinkle equal amount of confectioners' sugar over each and serve warm.

West African Pineapple Quencher

Makes 8 Servings of about 1/4 Cup.
1 Medium Pineapple, cut in half length wise, pared and cored. (Rinse and Reserve Peel)
4-6 Whole Cloves
1/2 Cup of Warm Water
Peel 1 Small Orange with Pith Removed.
1 Quart of Boiling Water
2 Tablespoons of Granulated Sugar
Cut one Pineapple half into small pieces and transfer pieces into large glass or stainless steel bowl, wrap remaining fruit and put in fridge for later. Stud Pineapple peel with cloves and add to bowl with Pineapple. In a small sauce pan bring 1/2 cup of water to a full boil and add orange peel and cook for 2 minutes. Drain peel and add to Pineapple. Add boiling water and sugar and combine with

Pineapple. Cover and let sit at room temperature for 24 hours. Strain and reserve the liquid, reserving the liquid and fruit without the peels. In the blender smooth the mixture and then pour into 2 quart pitcher. Cover and refrigerate. Serve over ice in chilled glasses.

I Got My Recipes From Weightwatchers New International Cookbook, 1985

Right now I am waiting on the batter to set up. The Pineapple Quencher is also setting up. It has to set up for 24 hours, which I didn't realize at first.

45 Minutes Later: Well, the Banana Fritters turned out pretty good. I burned the first few, but then I got the hang of it. They are like Banana Pancakes. When my parents came home, I had them taste the fritters. Their only complaint was that they weren't warm, but I couldn't help that they got home late!

May 19, 1996: Today, I strained the punch and then put it in the fridge. A few hours later, I tried it. It turned out I put too many cloves in and it was watery. It needed a stronger Pineapple taste. The Pineapple Peel probably would have made a difference. I will know better next time. My Mom and my Boyfriend agreed that it needed something more, but it was definitely drinkable.

May 27, 1996: I was going to make it one more time and then the third and last time for the in class. That is what I thought we were supposed to do. Then, in class, you said to try different recipes. I might have if I'd realized that earlier. That and I put off the project for too long. So, all I can do is prepare for Wednesday. PS Mom bought me a whole Pineapple and some bananas yesterday at the store. I am going to make more punch today and let it sit for 24 hours. Then put it in the fridge until time for class. Keep your fingers crossed it it turns out great this time!

(Mrs. Alemendinger wrote in pen that is was great!)

May 28, 1996: I've decided to make the Banana Fritters batter tonight. I won't have time tomorrow. I will leave the batter in the fridge until it is time to fry the fritters up. It should be okay for a day

or so.
Well, that is about it. Hopefully, everything will go right for class. I
am nervous about presenting it. I feel like I haven't done enough and
maybe this journal should have been longer? It might have been if
hadn't let time slip by me so fast. Next time, I won't put it off. I've
learned that much. I have also learned how much effort goes into
basic survival things like getting ingredients and cooking. Above all,
I learned how good African food is! (Mrs. Alemendinger wrote:
Right!) Grade 95%

June 3, 1996 Final 2pm to 3:48pm

History 518 Germany in the 20th Century

Instructor: Dr. Raymond Dominick
Office: Ovalwood 355
OSU Mansfield Fall 1998
Tuesdays and Thursdays 5-7pm

Texts: *Before The Deluge* by Fredrick, *Hitler and Nazi Germany* by Spielvogel and Germany *From Partition to Unification* by Turner.

Objectives:
1) To Evaluate Conflicting Interpretations of Germany's Past, trying to learn why participants and supposedly expert commentators disagree about aspects of German's History.
2) To practice posing and answering questions about the past
3) To become familiar with the tumultuous course of German's history in the 20th Century:

    A. The fractured legacy of earlier centuries
    B. The causes, course and outcome of WWI
    C. The Revolution of 1918 and 1919
    D. The Success and Failure of the Weimar Republic
    E. The extraordinary cultural achievements of the Weimar era, including film, drama, Literature, architecture, painting and music
    F. The nature of the Nazi's, the reasons for their rise and the character of the Reich that they established
    G. The causes, course and outcome of WWII.
    H. The Holocaust
    I. The post War occupation, partition and de-Nazi-fication
    J. The development of prosperous, capitalist democracy in West Germany
    K. The Green Movement
    L. The origins, nature and recent collapse of the Communist Regime in East Germany
    M. Re-Unification, trials of former official in East Germany, harassment of contemporary

Issues, fiftieth anniversaries, the 1998 National Elections and Other Contemporary issues as well as prospects for the future.

September 24, 1998 Introduction

Germans had a multitude of of identities. Some were Protestant and others were Catholic. There were wealthy bourgeois, blue collar workers and those in poverty. Most of the lower class was made up of immigrants or Polish and Turkish. Germany was fragmented and often prejudice. The North looked down on the South. Munich and Berlin citizens often made snide comments about each other.

Germany isn't very big. There are a lot of people in a a compressed space. It is maybe the size of Ohio, Indiana and Illinois. Where is Germany exactly? Its boundaries have been all over the map. It was once known as The Holy Roman Empire. Often its boundaries included non-German speaking areas like The Netherlands, Italy, Poland, Czechoslovakia and Switzerland among others. It was never centralized.

The Confederacy of Germany was comprised of Prussia and Austria fighting for dominance. They co-existed uneasily for years before war broke out in the 1860s. Prussia conquered and Bismarck became chancellor. This was during the time of the 2nd Reich Germany occupied parts of France and Russia during this time. This was known as The German Empire from 1871 until 1918.

In Russia the Romanov family was overthrown and there was a revolution. That revolution spread into Germany. They lost territory in Poland and Czechoslovakia. This led to World War I. After WWI we have the rise of the Third Reich and Adolph Hitler. Germany was defeated a second time during WWII. Germany was left quite a bit smaller without Poland, Czechoslovakia and Austria. Germany was also occupied by 4 countries after the war—England, America and France the West and in the East they were occupied by Russia.

Questions:
1) Where should Germany's boundaries be? How should the boundaries be drawn? By Culture? By Government? By War?
2) How Can Germany be kept from dominating and abusing its neighbors?

NATO was created to keep the Russians out of Europe and keep Germany from becoming too powerful again.

Germany now has many different Political Parties. Here are the Parties after 1890.

Social Democrats: This is similar to England's Labour Party and is for Welfare.

Center: Catholics whose agenda is to protect the Catholic Church's interests. It is usually 15- 20 percent of the votes from the population.

Progressives: Are a bunch of small groups. Down on votes.

National Liberals: Moderate Democrats. They don't have much influence and are revolution oriented.

Conservatives: Count for 10 to 15 of percent of the vote.

SPD: Want improvements

K: Represents Communism.

For most of the 20th Century Liberals had more votes while Conservatives ran the country.

The current 1998 Election was important. Helmet Kholes who was for Unions got 35.2 % of the votes. The Greens are pushing for Environmental Protection. The FDP are the Free Democrats. One key topic this election was also about Employment. 25 parties competed on Sunday. Schroder Won!

Back to the Past! Germans are often considered a war-like people. Were they responsible for WWII? Questions to consider:

1) Is there continuous aggressive impulse in Germany from the 1800s to WWII?
2) How did WWI get started?
3) What could have been done different during the revolution to create a healthier republic?
4) How did the Versailles Treaty weaken the Weimar Republic?
5) How did WWI effect The German people or steer Germany toward the 3rd Reich?

Was Bismarck an early Hitler? Bismarck had limited, modest goals, but not Hitler. Their differences were greater than their similarities. Bismarck wasn't focused on racial issues. Hitler was all about expanding its borders. Expansion was important for an Empire. France and England had created great empires. Germany was still small.

The problem was that they were relatively landlocked, so they were forced to attacked countries around them that were considered more civilized than those Africa and South America. Germany felt like they needed a navy to compete on the world stage. Germany also began to Militarize in order gain authority and respect.

William Lepkinect ran the biggest party before WWI. They were more peaceful and wanted to dismantle the army. There were many Germans who were for peace, but they often ended up in the concentration camps. Wilhelm I Kaiser didn't have power.

Prussia took over Germany. While Wilhelm called himself Emperor, the Chancellor had more power. There was a Federal Counsel of Bundersrat that had 26 Federal States. The Reichstag assured a universal suffrage for men. Women gained the right to vote in Germany after World War II. Social Democrats threatened the old Aristocracy and Monarchy. Nationalism seduced people away from the Socialist party.

Germany was enthusiastic for war. They believed that Russia was attacking them. Germany believed they were fighting in self-defense. Germany was trying to expand. Arch Duke Ferdinand as assassinated. His death served to dispose the discontent of foreign policy. Austria was failing. The original conflict was between Austria/Hungry and Serbia. The Serbs were angry with Austria and Hungry. Serbs were trying to withdraw. Austria wouldn't let them separate. The radical Serbs assassinated the Arch Duke Ferdinand to overthrow Austria. Austria struck back or counterattacked. The Austrian Ambassador went Germany for an alliance and Kaiser Wilhelm said yes.

The Kaiser wants foreign policy to be a success and believed in socialism. Germany miscalculated. They guessed Russia might jump in, however they didn't foresee France and the United Kingdom joining as well. The Austrians, Hungarians and Serbs were on the brink of revolution, as was Russia.

Austria went to war with Serbia with Germany backing them. France and Russia joined the effort to stop Germany. They were afraid of Germany's power. The US didn't officially declare war until 1917. Italy came in around 1915 to join France, Russia and the US even though they were supposed to be on Germany's side.

Politics were kind of like plate tectonics around the turn of the century. With the advent of Industrialization, monarchies were being overthrown. When we step back and look at the big picture, we see the Great War or the First World War building up over a long period of time.

So why did Germany lose WWI? Germany was blockaded in. They almost won in 1914. Then it was a stalemate. They were just killing each other with no real progress. Then there was the battle of Verdun. A million men were killed on a battlefield with no significant battle lines.

Russia was also landlocked. From 1916-1917 Russia was cracking. Which country cracked first? Russia cracked first. The Bolshevik Revolution took place and Germany was able to knock Russia out of the war.

The US entered the war just as Russia was leaving. US made an impact in the battle. They blunted the German offensive in 1918. There was a shift in power with fresh American Soldiers. Germans retreated out of friends. Germany and the Kaiser sues for peace.

Chronology of the German Revolution 1918-1919

September 29: Military High Command Demands Suit for Peace

October 5: Appointment of Prince Max as Chancellor and Confirmed by Reichstag

October 28: Onset of Mutiny at Kiel

November 7: Proclamation of a Republic In Munich

November 9: Proclamation of Republic In Berlin.

November 10: Ebert-Groener Deal

November 11: Germany Surrenders Unconditionally

November 12: Ebert appeals to all government employees to stay at their posts

December 16-20: Assembly of Councils calls for Early Elections

January 5-12: Spartacist Uprising in Berlin

January 19: Elections Held For Constituent Assembly

Spring 1919: Radical Uprising in Berlin, Soviet Republic and Counter Revolution in   Munich.

June 28: Signing of Versailles Treaty

July 31: Adoption of the Constitution at Weimar

September 29 1998 WWI: Defeat and Revolution

Armistice Day was on November 11, 1918. It was changed to Veterans Day later on.

So the Serbs were given Yugoslavia after the war. The Serbs and Crotes are still fighting each other.

How did WWI steer Germany toward WWII? Hitler grew up in Austria and detested it. He volunteered to be in the German Army. Many of the best and brightest Germans had been killed in the war. However, many of the surviving veterans of WWI became Top Nazi's. During the war Germany resorted to Socialism to get them through. They had no private economy. The Government had fed them a ton of propaganda. They were desensitized to violence and death.

In January of 1919 social democrats elected officials to write constitution. They had 75%of the votes. The Center Catholics were the runner up. The Communist Party was left out of the election. Male and females both did the Voting. Armistice was signed, but there was no treaty at first. The Treaty Diktat or Dictated Treaty was written by those elected to frame the constitution.

The Germans were shocked at terms and ready to go to war over it again. Groener and Hindenburg want to go to war rather than live with the terms of the treaty. The treaty was political suicide in their eyes. The people blamed the Social Democrats rather than those truly responsible. The Treaty was bad for Democracy and led the Germans to distrust Democracy for years to come.

The Terms of the Treaty: The Country of Germany lost part of their borders to Denmark, France, Poland and Russia. They lost all their colonies in Africa and the Pacific Islands. Austria wanted to join with Germany.

Germany's military was disabled. And the Germans were very upset about that and other unfair limitations. The Rhineland was occupied through 1930 and was unable to build a military presence. Russia built military equipment and shipped it to Eastern Germany.

Germany had to pay reparations for the damages. War Guilt Clause Article 231 forced Germany into taking responsibility for the War. They had War Crime Trials, but no one was convicted. Hitler dismantled the trials when he came to power.

Woodrow Wilson and the League of Nations came up with peaceful solutions. They were determined to prevent Germany from threatening Europe again. Germany couldn't join the League of Nations and neither could Russia.

Next week we will discuss the History of Jews in Germany and the Antisemitism that existed for a long time. Questions to Consider:

      1) Why were Jews the object of hatred?
      2) What worked against Democracy in Germany after WWI?
      3) Why were there revolutions in 1918 and 1919?
      4) Why did the leftists fail to support the revolution?
      5) Why didn't Ebert create an entirely new military?

October 1, 1998 Founding of the Republic

Weimar was pronounced Viamar. They created a Constitution and had a President elected by Votes. The Monarchy was eliminated. The President had a 7 year term that could be re-elected. A Chancellor was appointed.

Prepositional Representation was where they assigned seats according to percentage of people. The Prepositional Representation was more Democratic than the USA. Building Coalitions was difficult and the result was often unstable.

There were 9 Chancellors in like 4 years. See Ebert, Shedeman, Bauer, Muller, Fehrenbach, Wirth, Cuno, Luther, Marx, Brunning, Papen, Scheicher.

The President had Emergency Powers with Article 48. If the public is under any sort of threat or there is unrest, the president can do whatever he wants. Basically he could take over whenever he felt like it. Hindenburg was elected in 1925 and he was never a great friend of Democracy. Hindenburg invoked Article 48 and established a dictatorship.

Some Right Wing people wanted a dictatorship to rebuild their army and get revenge for WWI. In the Spring of 1920 Right Wings attempted a seizure of power in a Coupe De Ta. This coup de ta was remarkably in effectual though. Ludendorff was a part of it. He was tried and acquitted. The judges were on the side of the coup. The Anti-Democrats had NOT been purged. It was an incomplete revolution.

There was a General Strike where everyone had stopped working. President Ebert had called for this Strike. He ran off to Nuremberg or somewhere while it was happening though.

New Elections were held in 1920. Muller, who was a Centrists, became Chancellor. Social Democrats were blasted by voters. Radical Communists actually got a lot of votes. The Right Wing parties were growing in numbers and in strength.

Ratheneau was a Symbol of the Republic. His death was more important to Germany than the person who killed him The Republic was weakened by Assassinations. Many good people didn't want to enter into politics for fear of getting killed. These conspiracy theories overlapped with the *Freikorps*. The "Free Corps" was like our National Guard or Volunteer Military organization.

Then there was the problem of Runaway Inflation. The economy went from bad to worse. Money was basically worthless. Their money had been backed by gold, but then the government just kept printing money without anything behind it. They needed taxes for reparations and bills. Instead of taxing their citizens, they just printed more money. They took out loans to pay for the war and couldn't pay the loans back, so they printed yet more money.

In 1919 it was $9 American Dollar to $1 German Deutschmarks. By 1921 it was $1 American Dollar for $65 Deutschmarks. By 1923 it was $1 American Dollar for 4 Trillion Deutschmarks. At this point, they were desperate for goods and not money. Only a few people profited from this steep inflation. Profiteers made smart loans. People lost money getting loans from banks, so private loans were the way to go.

In 1924 there was a Pacifism movement. See Nie Wieden Kring.

October 6, 1998 Economics

The connection between Economics and Politics is very strong. The Economy often determines the fate of politicians. Hard times means a shaky Republic. Once the Economy stabilizes, then the Republic is stronger. The Great Depression was the Fall of the Republic in Germany.

Runaway Inflation and a large Deficit sunk the Economy. More than ¾ of the revenue was from loans. Deficits were shrinking in 1922, but War Reparations payments began.

Russia is doing this today. Will Russia become the new Germany?

There was a problem with Germany's new currency. They didn't have enough gold to back it. They also lived under the assumption that all property was Mortgaged property. They got International Package Loans from the USA. The US got war loan payments from England, France and other places. Germany wasn't paying England. Germany owed the US a ton of money.

Germany had Fiscal Discipline and worked hard to Balance the Budget. Interest Rates kept going up and the Government had to keep spending. Things were NOT running smoothly despite their best efforts.

The 1924 Elections brought a wave of Rebellion. The Election showed how unstable the Republic was. Social Democrats were getting less votes. The Anti-Democratic party (DNVP) was influencing the people. Alfred Hugenberg important. Voter turnout was 80%. The Nazi's got 6 to 7% of the vote.

Then there was the 1928 Election. The Nazi's got 2.6 of the votes. The Communists got like 1 out of 10 votes. The DNVP dropped way back. The DDP was down a little. The Social Democrats votes grew to around 30%.

The Foreign Policy was the same. Stresemann was the Rational Republican. He is the one who used the loophole article for the Chancellor. He tried to bury the hatchet with France. He was instrumental in the Treaty of Locanzno in 1925. There was an ominous side to the treaty. There was no promise to the Eastern Frontier. Teutonic Knights were seizing power in the East. The Kaiser had been interested in the East because it was his ancestor's home. Stresemann and the others had given up the idea of settling or controlling the East.

They began to co-operate with Russia. Hitler and Stalin would eventually carve up Poland and split it. Negotiations were secretly held between Russia and Germany. Armies had a lot to gain from this. Germany built industries in Russia so they could build airplanes and tanks. Both countries were outcasts and not in the League of Nations. They became unlikely allies. Publicly in 1922 it was announced there was a Treaty of Peace between Germany and Russia. 1924 through 1929 Germany's military spending doubled and that wasn't hidden. Other countries were aware that Germany was not complying completely with the treaties.

October 8, 1998 Weimar Culture

The Kaiser tried to control culture before WWI. Afterward, there was a new found freedom. 1920s in Berlin was a unique time. Culture and Art flourished. Before WWI there had been little to no innovation. The Kaiser had controlled all the art. He thought freedom was over used and not important. We had the DADA art movement, which believed art was private and chaotic. Later, the Dada movement spread to Paris.

Max Klinger pressed the limits of Art. He did the Blue Nudes. He did the Crucifixion. He had a rebellious theme. There was Kate Vollwitz practiced private patronage. There were the Berlin Sessions —group Sessions.

Erille Molde was an Anti-Semitic from Dresden. From the Group "Die Driuke." Molde was known for Impressionism and Expressioni-sm. There was Peter Gaye who was an Outsider/Insider from Viamar Culture.

Kandinsky was born in Moscow and Educated in Law and Physics, but he moved to Munich in 1908 and gave all that up. Pointillism and Impressionism were his favorite styles. He was trying to break with traditionalism and do art for art's sake.

Otto Dix, Max Beckman and George Groz were important artists. They depicted the gore of war, torture and rape. It was all part of the New Realism.

There were also plays and cabarets and three penny operas. There were new composers and plays at the theater.

In 1910 people fought over the modernization of music. Atonel Next or Atonel Expressionism was controversial. From 1914 until 1923 there was very little music at all. In 1924 the Twelve Tone Method was created. After 1933 Germany focused on American Music.

Emil Jannings was a Nazi actor who won an Oscar. Marlene Dietrich acted in The Blue Angel. We also have people like Einstein and Herman Hesse and Spengler coming out of this time.

There were Led Zeppelins too! Zeppelins were considered safer air travel than airplanes despite the crash of the Hindenburg in 1937. After the war all the blimps were destroyed because all the allies wanted them for payment. In 1928 wages in Germany rose over 20%. The war reparations lessened and they had more control over their economy.

This was also a time for youth groups. Some were harmless enough, but others were violent. Drugs like cocaine were rampant and crimes were on the rise. Pornography was also on the rise. Anyway, Hitler had been in prisoner, but what he got out in 1924, he joined one such violent youth group.

October 13, 1998 Beginning of the Nazis

Hitler was born April 20, 1899 in Austria. Adolf was the 4th child of his father's 3rd wife. He was the son of Clara Polzl and Alois Hitler. He did okay in Elementary School. Later his grades dropped. He left school in 1905 for two years. He was considered lazy and a dreamer. He preferred fantasy to reality. He was always impatient and quick to anger. In 1907 he pursued art in Vienna.

In 1913 Hitler moved from Austria to Munich to avoid Military obligations.

Hitler fought in WWI. Then he went to prison after the war. He got out of Prison in 1924. Hitler's book *Mein Kompf* was published. People latched on to his Manifesto. 1920 saw the Heil Salute being used by the Nazi's. 1921 Storm Troopers became police force of the Nazis.

Then came the election of Hindenburg. The attacks began in July. Goebbels hated Berlin. He respected vital hard working people, but he had a fanaticism and ruthlessness about him. He gave speeches and held rallies. He attacked Dr. Weiss, who was harmless, but a Jew.

The Nazi split into two factions in Berlin. The Party Chief Gregor Strassor. Others supported the SA Leaders or Storm Troopers. Kurt Daluege, Gautier and Ernest Von Sclange were important players.

Hitler was a short, unimpressive and ugly man. He was boring. But he was also a monster who was half insane. He was unable to speak and write German without error. He would ramble on about the loyalty of dogs. He was indecisive and made decisions at the last minute. He did, however, have a good sense of timing. He let his enemies destroy themselves.

Two people influenced Hitler: George Von Schonerer and Karl Leuger. Both were antisemitists. He took their policy and formed his own Nazi Party. The ex-Catholic monk Adolf Lanz founded the New Templars. He pulled Occultism, Nationalism and Antisemitism into a new Arisophy. See also Stefan George as well. Hitler began to use Propaganda to try and overthrow the Weimar Republic.

In the beginning the 50% of the Nazi's were 23 and Younger. Also they were mostly male. What few women had been involved were mostly withdrawn by 1923. A crisis in 1923 allowed the Nazi's to become a strong party. There was the Kampfbund or the March on Berlin. There was the Beer Hall Putsch Collapse. The turning point for the Nazi's was from 1928 until 1929. They concentrated on small building their forces in small towns—gaining support from the farmers who had economic difficulty.

With the exception of Goering, the Leaders of the Nazis were lower middle class who were looking to move up in the world. Workers were stable in their union. The Elite were drawn to the Nazis because they promised the return of the Monarchy. Interestingly, the Catholics were less drawn to Hitler than Protestants.

Questions for Next Week:
1) Did German Youth Education (Formal and Extra Curricular) make them especially right winged?
2) What was the influence of Vienna on Hitler?
3) What factions existed within the Nazis?
4) What kind of people were the early Nazis?
5) What was the appeal of the Nazis?
6) How did the Nazis plan to come to power?

October 15, 1998 Gleichschlatung

***Gleichschaltung* (**or in English **Coordination)** was in Nazi terminology the process of Nazification by which Adolf Hitler and the Nazi Party successively established a system of Totalitarian control and coordination over all aspects of German society and societies occupied by Nazi Germany "from the economy and trade associations to the media, culture and education"

Das Volk meant The Folks or Folkish. They were a powerful community who liked Americans. They believed in the Mythical Unity of the German People. They wished to exclude foreigners who were not "pure bloods." The DNVP was the biggest right wing group and their name was *Duetch National Volkish Party.* Hitler didn't invent the platform he would run on. He merely tapped into what was already there. However, he presented the ideas as his own and in a new style. His rise to power was more about style rather than substance.

Britany did her presentation on **The Psychopathic God** by Robert G. L. Waite (1977). Hitler had terrible childhood memories of his parents and their violent sexuality. His father was cold. He was a bit closer to his mother, although, he believed women to be the embodiment of evil. He was traumatized by having a missing testicle and by the fact that he never had much success in relationships with women. Hitler believed Medusa resembled his mother. And although Hitler promoted family values in public, he didn't appear to have any in private. He had a girlfriend Ava Braun who had tried to kill herself. Hitler was fascinated by the idea of suicide was this his draw to Ava?

How did Vienna affect him? He was rejected from the Art School in Vienna. He loved Art. Despite not getting into school, he stayed in Vienna up until the start of WWI. His adult personality and political perspectives were shaped by Vienna. There was a lot of antisemitism in Vienna. They were enough visibly distinct to make prejudice easy. He drank in the hatred. He believed in Antisemitism before the idea of Christianity and Christ. The Romans, among others, persecuted anyone they viewed as dangerous or rebellious.

Hitler hated horses, but he loved owning pictures of horses. His obsession with pictures of Stallions might have to do with his impotence. The book also book examined Hitler's Speeches and how Hitler lied all the time for tactical reasons.

Hitler thought of himself as the Second Coming of Christ. A psychopath doesn't think anyone or anything outside of the self is real. Was he aware of what he was doing? Was conscious or did have a conscience? Whatever the case, when Hitler and the Nazi's Christians came to power their rationale was NOT Christian.

Both of Hitler's parents were Austrian. There is evidence his Grandfather was Jewish. Did he project his hatred of his family onto the Jews? Maybe. A Nuremberg attorney discovered a black mail letter from his half-sister. The fact was Hitler's father was illegitimate and he wasn't sure of who is father (Hitler's Grandfather) was. His Grandmother had been employed in the house of a Jew. She was paid for 14 years by the family—perhaps because their son had fathered a son with her. When Hitler came to power he turned the home of his Grandmother into a Military base and destroyed any evidence of her impropriety.

In the 1890s some Jews wanted their own Nation State. This was Zionism. Religious based Antisemitism was fading. In Germany the sentiment was based on Nationalism and Racism. Racism alleges that Jews are genetically different or inferior. Nazi's viewed them as Subhuman. It is easier to inflict pain on others if you don't see them as human. The Jews were more or less scapegoats for the Germans to hate. Hitler believed Jews were evil and this evil had to be exterminated. It helped him make sense of his world even if there was no real grounds for his hatred. Plenty of Educated and Scientific people believed the Jews were evil as well.

Passionate German Nationalism meant hatred toward all other nations. The Pan Germanic League pushed Germans of Slavic Descent to 2nd Class Citizens. Vienna was the capital of a Multi-National Empire. 1/3rd of Vienna was German and 2/3rds were of other countries or of another ethnicity. This bigotry and prejudice was learned in Vienna. That attitude was Darwinism and Survival of the Fittest. It was brutal and cruel. This struggle to be the best made Hitler and made Germany.

The Climb to Power for Hitler was 1930 to 1933. In September of 1930 the Nazi vote rose from 800,000 to 6.5 Million. The Nazis used propaganda to gain support for their idea of Volksgemeinschaft or National Community via newspapers, radio and movies. Hitler and Hindenburg ran against each other in an election, but no one won. Hitler wooed industrial leaders and financial leaders. They had another election and Hitler won. Strausser was murdered and Hindenburg signed over the Chancellor position to Hitler.

October 20, 1998 Culture and Society in Nazi Germany

Hitler and Stalin: Parallel Lives by Alan Bullock is 1991 book we discussed in class. The title and structure of the book refer to the ancient Greek write Plutarch and his *Parallel Lives*. Bullock states that it is their childhood roots that led them to such poisonous power.

Hitler was shaped by his parents, shaped by Vienna and shaped by WWI. The German party was where he was sent to spy. He rallied workers to the National Cause. He tried to analyze why Germany lost WWI and came up with the Public Program.

1. Nationalism was key to being cohesive and motivated.

2. In order to start a new war he was going to have to get people to rally against the Versailles Treaty.

3. Appeal to the idea of living space or *Lebensraum.* It was important for the German people to feel like they didn't have enough space and that they were entitled to more.

4. Racism. Only pure Germans deserved to be in Germany. Jews and other aliens needed to be pushed out or exterminated. Read Der Sturner about the idea of specific targeted murders.

5. Put the Common Good before Individual Good was important for accomplishing these goals. Doing it in the name of Socialism would have given them more freedom to violate one group of people in the name of the other. This was a means to an end.

National Socialism developed into Fascism. The Traits of Fascism:

1) Cult of Personality and Charisma of Leader
2) The Need of the Nation put in the highest order
3) Militaristic
4) Male Chauvinism is rampant
5) Totalitarianism. Everything For The State
6) Corporate Economy
7) Anti-Liberal
8) Anti-Communist

Eric Fromm wrote a book *Escape From Freedom* about the Psychology of not being self-determined. Things were not collectively owned, but bureaucrats were put into place to dictate everything. Profits were high and strikes were non-existent. Rape was NOT used as a tool to control people—at least not on a National Level. Fascism was against FREE anything though. The liberals wanted free speech and free voting, etc.

Hitler was more style than substance. People claimed bright blue eyes were powerful. He called them Medusa Eyes. Most people agree his mustache was ugly though. He kept repeating the phrase that Germany was now AWAKE! Leiner Riefenstahl directed the 1933 movie of Hitler's Nazi Rally where the humans looked like thousands of ants.

While Hitler and some of the SS officers were Catholic, most of the Nazi party was Protestant. There were only like 55 people in the Nazi party when Hitler first joined. The ranks grew to millions. They recruited in rural areas and small towns. People in the cities were less supportive.

Key Players in the Nazi Party:

Rudolf Hesse: He flew to England and was a WWI veteran. He wasn't arrested, but volunteered to go to prison. He became the Deputy Feur—as Hitler's Personal Secretary.

Herman Goering or The Red Baron. He was head of the Air Force and part of the 4 year plan. He married a rich aristocrat and was addicted to drugs—morphine and cocaine.

Joseph Goebbels was not a WWI veteran. He was disabled. He joined the Nazi Part y in 1922 and worked his way up. He was not from Bavaria, but Berlin. He was originally left wing socialist. He put his weight behind Hitler despite not agreeing with his politics. He was a very powerful leader in charge of Propaganda.

Henrich Himmler never came to power through the party. He was a chicken farmer who trained in sales. He had no real distinguishable accomplishments, but he did end up controlling the police power. He believed in biological racism.

Ernst Rohm was a Beer Hall Member. He fled from the countryside. He went to Bolivia for 5 years. In the 1930s Hitler persuaded him to come back and take over the SA or Sturm Abteilung (Storm Troopers). The SS stood for Schtaffelin and had only a few hundred members. It was smaller than the SA Army. The SA had some 2 million troops by the war. The SS grew to Millions by the war. They demanded proof of racial purity back 4 generations. The SS joined to serve Hitler, not necessarily Germany. The SS was originally Hitler's Bodyguards, but they became a separate Military Arm. Their slogan was *"Sword and Plow" "Fight and Obey"* and *"Blood and Honor."* The new German Nation was all about the Racial Elite.

The Plan to come to power was originally a collaboration with the Bavarian Government. The Bavarian Military originally opposed him, but then he had a mass march and twisted their arm. He hoped the Beer Hall Putch would accomplish his goal. It failed completely and he was jailed for treason for a year.

The Industrialists needed to contribute power, so Hitler met with the leading Industrialists and promised to keep them in power. He gave them money and said as he rose to power they would get more business. A few actually did give him money. Most Industrialists gave money to the DNVP instead. They were hostile to the Weimar Republic.

So what brought Hitler to Power? The loss of WWI and the bad deal Germany got with the Treaty of Versailles set up a lot anger, resentment and general discontent. The Great Depression and Economic issues led to desperation among the German people. The Nazi vote soared from 3% in 1928 to 18% in 1930 to 37% in 1932. Next week we will discuss what happened once they gained power.

October 22, 1998 Nazi Foreign Policy

Hindenburg surrounded himself with people who hated Democracy. Most Germans were tired of Democracy. Then Article 48 passed. Bloomburg let Goebbels take over. Hitler became Chancellor. There was a big parade and then Shoeburg was exiled to Paris. Hitler then promised heads would roll. 150 "Enemies of the State" were rounded up. Nazis burned all the books that Goebbels disliked. They called it Entartete Kunst or Degenerate Art. They raided museums and got rid of Van Gogh and many others. Most people went about their daily lives, but there were a few who became Anti-Hitler.

Gleichschlatung continued and the Nazis continued to eliminate any opponents. They were afraid of trade unions and the like. The forcefully eliminated other parties. They purged. Hitler simply wanted Tyrannical power. He used the Nazi ideologies for his own personal gain.

The s**wastika** is a **geometrical figure**and an ancient religious icon in the cultures of **Eurasia**. Swastika is used as a symbol of divinity and spirituality in Indian religions. It also appears in Greece, Tibet, Japan and America. It is a charm against the evil eye. By 1910 it had been appropriated to denote the Aryan Race.

Despite the fact the fact that Hitler was elected to create an economic recovery, there was no stable economic plan. 5.6% of people were unemployed in 1932. In the following years it dropped to 3.7%. More people were employed, but wages were low. Small producers and consumers were hurt by this unstable economy. The New Plan involved increasing State Control and Increasing German trade. Hitler began implementing the Lebensraum or Living Space Expanse Program.

The SS began overseeing baptisms and weddings in order to make sure it was in accordance with the pure race policy. However, the churches often provided hurdles for the political policies Hitler promised Freedom of Religion, but it was mostly a freedom to practice protestant Christianity because it was vague enough not to be a threat. When the church protested about anything, Hitler would go on an Anti-Christian rant. Distrust began to develop.

Jews were prevented from taking any government jobs. They were pushed into Ghettos. Then they were shipped into Camps. By 1935 it was illegal to be a Jew in Germany. In addition to Jews, between 2500 and 3500 political opponents were placed in concentration camps. Other countries heard about these camps and were not happy about them, but they didn't realize the extent and didn't interfere. The Pope actually supported Nazi Germany at first.

Stephanie did her report on Nazi Culture. She read a collection of articles from the 1920s and the 1930s. How were common people affected? The local school curriculum were replaced with religious instruction and Nazi Ideologies. They were taught *"How To Spot A Jew"* among other things. Pseudoscience and not actual science was taught.

Gym Class or Physical Training was a large part of education as well. Cripples weren't allowed to progress in higher levels of education since they couldn't pass Gym. Welfare was threatened to be taken away if people refused to participate.

Parents were angry and voiced their dismay at local town meetings. Hitler's Youth Clubs were mandatory after school activities. All Radio Programs, Play Productions and Movies had to be approved of by the Nazi Party.

Women were sent to farms to work. Government Service was required before they could attend college. The Universities were only allowed to admit people of the Aryan Race. It was a Volk State. No classes for Jews or any other undesirable.

The Nazis wanted to go so far as to eliminate the Old Testament of the Bible, but the Christians disagreed. Overall, there was much censorship and burning of books. Girl Scouts became the Girl's Corps for Hitler. Everything was Militarized.

Jean discussed the book They *Thought They Were Free* Milton Sanford Mayer. It explored why people in general are vulnerable to Totalitarianism.

"What happened here was the gradual habituation of the people, little by little, to being governed by surprise; to receiving decisions deliberated in secret; to believing that the situation was so complicated that the government had to act on information which the people could not understand, or so dangerous that, even if the people could not understand it, it could not be released because of national security. And their sense of identification with Hitler, their trust in him, made it easier to widen this gap and reassured those who would otherwise have worried about it."--from Chapter 13, "But Then It Was Too Late"

October 29, 1998 Midterm

November 3, 1998 The Holocaust

Meinkampf outlined his basic plan, but no one took it seriously. The Jews made up around 1% of the population, but that was still ½ a million people. 37,000 Jews fled Germany, but that was less than 1/10th of the population. Jews thought of themselves as German and many had no place to go.

From 1933 to 1935 Jews were discriminated against. Zionism was NOT popular in Germany in the least bit. Jews were not allowed to be Journalists or anybody of importance in society. Jewish doctors could only work on Jewish Patients. In 1933 Germans called for a Boycott of Jewish Businesses. Storm Troopers began standing outside of Jewish Businesses—discouraging people. Random arrests and beatings also began to take place regularly. This sparked international outrage and the Nazis backed off a bit.

Christian Grandparents had to be shown on both sides of your family. If you were even 1/4th Jewish or had just one Jewish ancestor, you weren't considered a true German. You were called a Mischlinger or of Mixed Blood.

In 1935 Jews given a specific definition and were considered outlaws. Expropriation occurred from 1933 to 1935. There was the **Kristallnacht** November of 1938. The name Crystal Night comes from the shards of broken glass that littered the streets after the windows of Jewish-owned stores, buildings and synagogues were smashed. The Germans said the Jews were responsible for the damage and took about 20% of their money as tax. Over 100 Jews were killed that night. The rest—somewhere between 20 to 30 thousand—were placed in Ghettos to specific parts of the cities. There was almost no resistance in the ghettos in Poland until the end of 1942,

Deportation to other countries began in 1933 until around 1938. Desperate Jews sold their businesses and tried to leave. Those who fled to Austria were no better off because Germany soon annexed Austria and began destroying their Jewish population was well. In 1938 and 1939 they were shipped to concentration camps. Extermination began in 1940 and 1941.

The plan was outlined in a paper entitled "How To Solve The Jewish Question." Anyone sent to these camps were starved, beaten and often tortured. They were often subject to medical experiments. Nazi doctors asked questions like *"How long does it take to freeze to death?"* and *"How much compression can a body take"*. Men and Women were sterilized. They injected people at the camps with new deadly viruses, among other things. The weak were often lead to the gas chambers right away. They used a mixture of carbon dioxide, Zyklon B and Hydrogen Cyanide in the Gas Chambers.

Jehovah Witnesses objected and took a stand. When they refused to join the army they were shot on the spot. Political Prisoners were re-educated and eventually released. The Jews went from the minority in the concentration camps to the majority before they started putting them in gas chambers.

The Holocaust was also known as the Shoah. Some six millions Jews had been exterminated from 1941 until 1945. Some were shot, but most were gassed. From the end of 1941, the Germans built six extermination camps in occupied Poland: Auschwitz II (established October 1941), Majdanek October 1941) Chełmno (December 1941), Bełżec (1942), Sobibór (1942), and Treblinka (1942); the last three are known as the Operation Reinhardt camps

England and France weren't sure what do about all of this. They knew of his plans, but didn't think he would put it into action. They didn't want to be alarmists and get in a war over nothing. World War I had taken a great toll on everybody they didn't want to see another huge loss of life. They believed, for a long time, Hitler would demand a revision in the Versailles Treaty is all.

When the Allied Soldiers arrived at the camps years later they found men, women and children starving to death and mass graves, they were horrified. They had no idea the conditions in the camps were that bad!

Questions to Consider For The Final:
1) What accounted for the German Military Success?
2) What and Where was the turning point for WWII?
3) Why did Hitler break the Nonaggression Pact and Invade the Soviet Union?
4) Was Hitler's command over his army absolute and complete?
5) What was Public Opinion in the US, UK, France and USSR?
6) How did the German's Exploit Resources of Conquered Territories
7) To what extent was the regular army involved in war crimes?

There were government announcements over the radio and in movies in Germany about what was happening, but not much. Many supported Hitler in for his Economic and Foreign Policies. Most Germans liked the idea of expansion. There was a select few who did protest what was happening in their own country, but they had not been successful in assassinating Hitler or overthrowing the Nazis

Ludwig August Theodor Beck (29 June 1880– 20 July 1944) was a German general and Chief of the German General Staff during the early years of the Nazi regime in Germany before **World War II**. Ludwig Beck never became a member of the **Nazi Party**, though in the early 1930s he supported **Adolf Hitler**'s forceful denunciation of the Versailles Treaty and his belief in the need for Germany to rearm. Beck had grave misgivings regarding the Nazi demand that all German officers swear **an oath of fealty** to the person of Hitler in 1934, though he believed that Germany needed strong government and that Hitler could successfully provide this so long as the Führer was influenced by traditional elements within the military rather than by the **SA** and **SS**. He was in secret Negotiations with England and France against Hitler during the war. He tried to bomb Hitler, but was unsuccessful. He was killed after the failed attempt at assassination.

Germany withdrew from The League of Nations. Then Hitler annexed Austria and had access to Czechoslovakia. Mussolini mobilized his troops at the boarder of Austria, but nothing came of it.

From the beginning Europe failed to control Hitler. He expanded and they did nothing despite inside information..

Germany then took over part of the Rhineland on June 18, 1935. If would France had stopped him from invading then there probably have been a WWII. France thought if he was appeased, Hitler would stop attacking. As of 1936, France actually had a bigger army than Germany. France later installed a Maginot Line of bunkers on land and battleships at sea, but Hitler went around them.

Also during this time England or Great Britain took over Palestine. The Arabs were also angry at the Jews. Italian Fascist Mussolini attacked part of Africa. Hitler helped Italy and Spain. Spain had a civil war which led to Fascist Franco take over. Hitler and the Russian Leader Stalin agreed not to attack each other at first, but later Germany did, in fact, attack Russia. Germany attacked Northern France on June 5th.

France and England drew their line in 1939. They made friends with Stalin, who was growing fearful of invasion from Germany. Hitler and Stalin made a nonaggression pact, but that didn't last.

England's Primer Minister Winston Churchill called for action after a number of failed negotiations with Hitler. Hitler would make promises and act as if everything were okay, but then go about his business creating chaos across Europe. When called out about attacking Poland on September 1, 1939, Hitler claimed Poland attacked Germany first.

Churchill knew that Great Britain spent about the same amount on their Military as Germany. He felt they could win a war against Germany. They had try anyway. No one wanted a German Empire. So, the war began in earnest when England and France declared War on September 3, 1939.

America joined later, after the bombing of Pearl Harbor by Japan in December 7, 1941. Hitler declared war on American earlier than that, but never attacked. He was mad that the US had provided Aid to England and France. The US was still operating under the Isolationist Theory and was trying to stay out of another World War, but did answer the call for some aid The US became entangled in the war, but eventually poured everything they had into it once they were directly attacked by Japan.

So where did Japan come in? They were not Aryan. Japan was at war with Russia, although they didn't officially declare war against each other until WWII broke out. Germany and Japan teamed up against Russia because they were both Anti-Communist. During WWII Japan invaded Korea. In 1937, Japan invaded China.

November 12, 1998 Military Defeat

Questions For The Final:
1) Why didn't Europe and America do more to prevent the Holocaust? Could they have done anything?
2) What were the steps taken to eliminate the Jews from Germany and then German occupied Countries?
3) Was there any Jewish resistance? If so, why wasn't it more effective? What could they have done, if anything?
4) What was the significance of the Holocaust in Modern History? How has it affected the world from then (1930s) until now (1990s almost 2000s)?

Germany had success early on. Poland provided little resistance. They had taken over in less than two weeks. Germany moved around Frances Mignot Lines. They had tanks that plow over the defensive lines. Paris surrendered on June 22 of 1940.

London was never completely taken over, but they took major damage. They also used blitzkrieg attacks from the air and they bombed a great deal of London before the end of the war. The Germans were able to use planes equipped with guns and bombs to take out strategic locations. In addition to those locations, Hitler managed to kill thousands of civilians.

England attacked back with their own tanks and planes. Getting to Germany by tank was difficult, however. England did damage to strategic German locations using planes mostly. The British Planes were built better than the German planes. The British were definitely better in the air fights. For every plane shot down by Germany, England managed to take two of Germany's planes. The British also developed radar to help them detect incoming planes.

In August of 1940 the British were desperate enough to plan a direct attack on Berlin. They used the technique of firebombing, which destroyed a large portion of the city and killed a lot of people. 30,000 people died. Was this a war crime? Maybe.

French aided with Military Intelligence and the use of Spies. Their army was inept at coordinating attacks with England though.

The turning point of the war was in 1940 when England broke Germany's secret code. Germany didn't know England knew their code though.

Operation Barbarossa ended on June 22, 1941. Russia was nearly knocked out of the War. They had more men and more tanks than Germany, but Russia wasn't enemies with all of Europe like Germany. Germans attacked Russia during the winter, which was a mistake. Many Germans died of starvation and exposure during the long winter. Eventually troops reached Stalingrad, but many surrendered in January of 1942.

Rommel led the Africa Korps, but was defeated in Africa in the Fall of 1942. He broke through Egypt and captured Torbruck. German submarines attacked the British Ships. Rommel was defeated in October. American and British troops moved in and pushed back the lines in the South. Russia attacked and pushed back the lines in the North. England held up their line in their line in the West.

Paris was liberated by the US and British troops on August 1, 1944. British and American troops were moving in on Germany. On January 16, 1945 Hitler and Eva Braun went into hiding in a bunkers. He began acting bizarre in his final days. He was on a ton of drugs though! Anyway, he married Eva on April 29th and he and then Eva kill ed themselves on April 30th. By May 7th Germany surrendered unconditionally.

November 19, 1998 After The War

Questions For Final:
1) Why were there two Germanys and not one? Why was Germany divided as it was into 4 Zones of Occupation?
2) What was the De-Nazification and how was it implemented?
3) What were the objectives of the Allies after the war?
4) What was the public perception of defeat in 1932 vs 1918?
5) How was the list of defendants decided at the Nuremberg Trial?

Sadly, after WWII there were Holocaust deniers. They say only a few thousand Jews died and they didn't die in gas chambers.

Revisionists, as they are often called, don't believe the blueprints for the camps that were found. The blueprints clearly show gas chambers on them.

On September 5, 1996, Holocaust denier David Irving sued Lippstadt and her publisher Penguin Books for libel in an English court for characterizing some of his writings and public statements about Holocaust denial in her book *Denying the Holocaust.*

What were the objective of the Allies after the War? Different Countries had Different Objectives. Americans wanted to keep Germany from starting another war. So how did they propose to do that? The USA believed in a United Nations to resolve international conflicts. They wanted to De-Militarize, De-Industrialize and De-Centralize Germany as well. However, other countries didn't want to punish Germany again like they did with the Treaty of Versailles. The harsh treaty backfired in many people's opinion.

De-Nazification was an attempt to remove Nazis and Nazism. They removed all powerful people from power and did away with National Socialism. They worked hard to replace ideas of the Nazi Dictatorship with ideas of Democracy. It was a re-education effort at each of the zones of occupation. Some people wanted to take the Nazis out and shoot them all, but it was felt that was something the Nazis would do. So, it was decided that they would be put on trial and held responsible for their crimes.

It was difficult to remove all the Nazis from their jobs, but they tried. They let some of the little fish go in order to focus on the major players. However, there were 106 cases tried in Germany by 1958. They had a total of 6,000 convictions! Major Nazis like Hitler, Himmler and Goebbels committed suicide. Other that were left were tried at Nuremberg: Goring was sentenced to death, Hesse was given a life sentence, Funk was given a life sentence, Spear got 20 years, Frank was sentenced to death, Von Papen went free due to double jeopardy, Ribbentrop was sentenced to death, Jodi was given a life sentence, Rosenberg was sentenced to death, Von Neurath got 15 years, Doenitz got 10 years and Papen got an 8 year sentence. At Nuremberg it was decided that just following orders is NOT an excuse for what they did. Other countries followed suit and had their own war crimes trials.

The Public was surprised by Germany's defeat after WWI. In 1945 Germany (and the rest of the world) was relieved and happy for the surrender after WWII. Russians retaliated violently. Soldiers

raped some 2 million women in Germany. Russia claimed Eastern
Germany (Eastern Berlin) for their own and occupied it.

Policy makers knew that Russia was going to pose problems.
The question arose in 1946 about how to handle them. Russia's
continued presence was part of the reason the US stayed in Germany,
but it was also for Economic Reason. Western Germany (Western
Berlin) was divided between France.

Marshall Plan came from Marshall who was the Secretary of
State of the US. The US helped rebuild France, Italy and England.
Russia did not get help from the US. Russia wanted to take over all
of Berlin, so it they were blockaded by a wall in 1949. West
Germans, The US and Britain were all against Communism and thus
The Soviet Union. In 1945 Germany was our enemy, but by 1949 we
were friends. The US needed Germany.

In 1947 Germany had a Minister-President. In 1948 there was an
Economic Council, which acted like Quasi-Parliament. Some Allies
were happy to see their effort at self-governance and some were
afraid it would be a threat to unity. Basic law was called
Grundgesetz, Bundersrat and Bundestag. We had the German
Democratic Republic in the East and The Federal Republic of
Germany in the East. Other things that came out of this time was the
Autobahn and a Black Market.

The Soviet Union controlled East Germany. There had a been a
Communist Movement in Germany before WWII, but Hitler had
stamped it out. Some still supported it. After the War East Germany
was very much under Communist Influence. The Ulbricht Era was
the 1950s in East Germany so named for Ulbricht. East Germany
worked on Socialization and Industrialization during this time.
Wages were low and East Germany's purchasing power wasn't very
good. There were food shortages, etc.

November 24, 1998 Socialism and Communism

Socialism and Communism have a lot in common. Both deal
with the working class and class struggle. The biggest difference is
that in Communism the wealth is collected and divided up evenly.

Karl Marx and Fredrich Engels, who were German, co-authored
a book on Socialism and Communism. Marx and Engels both had a
strong Jewish Heritage, but they rejected religion as adults. The truth
is that some form of Socialism would have existed in Germany

without the Soviet Union. The Soviet Union took their ideas from the German authors, in fact.

Leninism and Marxism agree that Economics drive history. They agreed the elite classes just got smaller and that not just the elite should own the means of production. The working class was key to a successful economy. There was supposed to be no jails and no government. However, someone had to oversee the distribution. The leaders ended up being corrupt and hoarding a great deal of resources. In any case, the workers were more interested in creating Unions than Communism.

Communism was supposed to get rid of greedy Monarchs who owned everything. It was supposed to make things equal, but it didn't. Communism ended up being just as oppressive the monarchy, if not more so. Marx demanded political equality. Leninist Communism was not equal. Marxist-Leninist or Stalinist was an oppressive form of Communism. The oppression was felt in the USSR as well as East Germany.

Ulbricht wanted a single party dictatorship in East Germany. He was angry that Communists had been put in Concentration Camps alongside Jews. He wanted to make sure that didn't happen again. However, he managed to create a totalitarianism government similar to Hitler's anyway. He employed the Stasi like Hitler. There were 1 million informants. Defection to West Germany was punishable by death. Despite all this, very few people resisted. They were intimidated into obedience.

Both Nazism and Communist Totalitarianism 1) Had Secret Police 2) Demanded Uniformity 3) Had Control of the Media and used it for Propaganda.

The Berlin Wall caused lots of problems. In 1958 food rations were lifted and prices were jacked up. 15,000 farms were deserted in the East and people moved to the West. On August 13, 1961 there were soldiers with guns posted along the wall to keep people from defecting.

East Germany didn't do away with Religion like USSR. They maintained mostly Protestant Churches. There were very few Catholic Churches. Church attendance dropped overall though. Before the war it was at 92%. After the war, only 36% of Germans went to Church in East Germany.

Socialist Parties in Europe have found more success than Communist ones. Currently Norway, Sweden and England have followed some Socialist models with great success. The Labor Party in England has much support from the public.

The SPD or Socialist Public Democratic Party wanted Reunification with Eastern Germany. They believed that Socialism wasn't to blame for Hitler and the Nazis, but the decadent Capitalism of the 1920s.

Different Structures of Government:

Hollow Shell: Had A Constitution and Looked Democratic, but was not truly one.

SED Party: Person Head of Power or General Secretary had the Real Power. It was a committee of men or a Political Burro. Burro was chosen by 100 members of the Party.

Democratic Centralism: Free Discussion and then the decision is made by the party.

The Party is Never Wrong Though.

The Term chauvinistic was created in 1920 to describe Stalin, Nazis and East German Communism. In theory, Communism isn't particularly sexist or chauvinistic.

What did the Germans think of their new governments? They really didn't do surveys and not everyone could vote. In 1953 there was one major revolt. Stalin had died and there were protests over upped work quotas. The revolt failed and produced no improvement because Russian tanks rolled in. At least 21 East Germans were killed, maybe more. There were other protests in other countries though. 1956 Protest in Hungary. In the 1960s there was a Protest in Czechoslovakia. In 1981 Protest in Poland. The US and other countries didn't intervene for fear of getting involved in a war with Russia. Nuclear War was fear throughout the whole cold war.

Even during the conflict with Korea on the 1950s, other countries hesitated to give Germany an army. Chancellor Brandt came to power in West Germany. He was Social Democrat. He signed the Warsaw Treaty in December of 1970. He was given a Nobel Peace Prize for Avoiding War. In 1974 he resigned. Helmut Kohl took office. In 1984 Richard Von Weizoaker became the Federal President. Foreign Minister Genscher had more power though.

In 1958 about 28% of Germans believed Germany would reunite. By 1980 that was down to just 3%. In the 80s they had all but given up. But East Germans were unhappy with their inferior economy. Yeah, it was better than USSR, but it was worse than West Germany and other countries. And the East was heavily restricted as far as travel was concern. There weren't many people able to travel between the East and the West.

Christa Wolfe was probably the most famous writer to come out of East Germany. She wrote *The Quest for Christa T, Cassandra* and *Medea*.

December 1, 1998 West Germany

Questions for the Final:
1) How did Democracy take root in Germany?
2) How did the Economy of FGR Recover so Spectacularly?
3) What was the Foreign Policy of FGR and why did it develop that way?
4) What were the direct repercussions of the building of the Berlin Wall both domestically and internationally?
5) How and why to the Socialist Democratic Party change?

Democracy took root because they had Allied Tutelage and they learned from past mistakes. They had Economic Prosperity and their Political Parties Evolved and Grew. They did away with Article 48 and Senators were directly elected. The State level Government was put back in place. The State place an important role because the State is usually in charge of the courts, education, the police force and the prison system. They also created a Federal Constitutional Court that acted like the US Supreme Court.

How did the Economy recover spectacularly? There was no downturn from 1950 until 1980. In the 1960s Unemployment was under 1%. Wages kept going up. Automobile manufacturing went up. They made more cars than Japan and were #2 in the world. Spending money on food went down while spending money on clothes and travel went up. Germans actually had savings. They used the US model and welcomed new technology.

Germany has created a successful mix of capitalism. Germany exported 1/3rd of its products. The elimination of tariff barriers helped. They moved from Government owned businesses to privately owned business, however the Government would intervene from time to time to make sure that the rich didn't get ALL the money. They implemented comprehensive job training and health insurance.

Germany was a big proponent of Nuclear Power in the 70s and 80s. They even contributed to Pop Culture beginning in the 1980s. German International Hit Songs include: *99 Luftballons.* Nena, 1983, *Rock me Amadeus.* Falco, 1989, Wind *of Change.* Scorpions, 1990, *Rock You Like a Hurricane.* Scorpions, 1984 and *Du Hast. Rammstein*, 1997.

A number of things happened in the 80s that lead to the ultimately Reunification of East and West Germany. Part of that was the economic downturn that came with the Oil Crisis, among other things. We will discuss that next week.

December 3, 1998 Unified Germany

Neue Ostpolitik ("new eastern policy"), was the normalization of relations between the Federal Republic of Germany (West Germany) and Eastern Europe, particularly the German Democratic Republic (East Germany) beginning in 1969. Influenced by Egon Bahr, who proposed *"change through **rapprochement"** in a 1963 speech at the **Evangelische Akademie Tutzing**, the policies were implemented beginning with Willy Brandt, fourth Chancellor of the FRG from 1969 to 1974.

In the 80s things took a downturn. There was a housing shortage, outdated cars and higher divorce rate. OPEC Oil Prices skyrocketed. This caused the collapse of the German Democratic Republic. The Soviet hold on the world was weakening and collapsing as well. Gorbachev came to power and begin Perestroika and Glasnost. Economic and Political changes or problems created a perfect storm and a bloodless revolution.

Trade began to increase between East and West Germany to make up for some of the shortages. Eventually the USSR let go of its iron grip on East Germany.

All of these issues came to a head in 1989. Demonstrations and Protests took place all fall. On November 9th they opened the wall up for free travel between the East and West, which led to the Germans knocking down portions of the wall. Eventually, the wall was demolished. Free Elections were held and East and West were unified.

The wall wouldn't have been possible if people hadn't have lost their fear of Mother Russia. They wouldn't have been able to come down without the support of the church. The Humanists, Marxists and Green Party all played a role in making Reunification Possible.

West Germany's population increased in the 1960s. It leveled off in 1970s. By the 1980s it had begun to shrink. There were some ten Million Immigrants had come to West Germany after WWII. Germany actually has a rather large Turkish Population. Germany doesn't deny immigrants benefits, but you do have to have ancestors in Germany to be considered a Citizen. East Germany had a steady increase in population despite some people fleeing to West Germany.

Part of the decrease in population was due to the availability of The Pill in the 1960s. They felt the Feminist Movement in Germany. It was actually quite powerful there. In fact, Germany is now far more progressive than the US where Women's Rights are concerned.

The German Green Party emerged from The Citizens Initiative and APO. It was a Grassroots movement. They rallied to get playgrounds built and protested Nuclear Power Plants. Eventually their party grew with numbers now in the 10s of Thousands.

SDS or Student For Democratic Society played a key role. Students at University have taken up the cause. They protested the Vietnam War and were for Conserving the Environment. Many of them are Radical Leftists, but they reject Lenin and Stalin.

The Founding Principles of the Green Party:

    Ecological: Limit Urban Growth

    Social: Belief in Taking Care of Their Own. Take Care of Planet

    Political: Nonviolence and Grassroots Democrats

The Green Party had members elected to office in 1977. They had 3% to 5% of the vote. The Elections were publicly funded, which meant more votes=more money.

Foreign Policy included an Economic Treaty between Italy, France, Luxembourg and Germany. They Eliminated Tax Tariffs an were able to trade with Norway, England, Portugal, Sweden, Finland and Austria as well. Germans were able to squire through peaceful means what they never could through violence. Germans were able to travel across Europe with just one passport. Europe created the Euro, so Germany used the Euro as well as the German Mark.

Germany has created their own Military. They felt they need a defense in case they were attacked. They considered Nuclear Weapons as the US and Russia built up their arsenal, but there were many protests in Germany against the development and use of said Nuclear Weapons.

December 8, 1998 Problems and Prospects

We watched a video of the news coverage of the fall of the Berlin Wall. On November 10th there were still people on top of the wall. Nothing was being done to prevent them from going over it despite it still being illegal.

Dave from class was in the service at the time and he actually witnessed it. There were fireworks on December 31st. Dave didn't leave Germany until August of 1990. Dominic, our professor, was in Germany in 1987 to 1988 and again in 1995. He didn't witness the actual fall, but he was there for the excitement before and after.

Possible Futures after the Dissolution of the German Democratic Republic.

1) Reassertion of the Repression via Coup from German Communists.
2) A Third Way where the GDR remains an Independent Force in a loose confederation of German States.
3) There could be a merger with the West under the FGR, which is what actually happened.

German underwent a 3rd Revolution. East and West Germany's shared history made the Revolution Possible. The Merger made Economic stressors for both East and West, but mostly the West. West Germany had to provide for 16 million more Germans.

1990 to 1997 some 4% to 5% of Germany Gross National Domestic Product went toward rebuilding East Germany. Part of that included cleaning up the Pollution Problem the East Had.

Helmut Kohl promised no new taxes, but he lied. About 2 out of 3 Industrial jobs were eliminated in East Germany. They just couldn't compete with West Germany. Many people migrated West even after the wall came down.

There was the property issue. Property claims conflicted after the division. People lost properties when they ran or moved. Now they wanted the land back. Kohl said the owners in the West could get their land back in the East. One guy committed suicide over this issue.

Border Guards who shot some 280 people were held responsible for their actions. They were charged and convicted of their crimes. Germany also issued Poland an apology for past behavior.

East German University Professors were forced to become Communist Party Members. After Reunification half of the Professor were fired. The other half abandoned their Membership to the Communist Party.

East and West had very different views on abortion. In the East they were able to obtain an abortion without a problem while the West required a medical reason. Unified Germany had to find a middle ground.

East and West had very different views on religion as well. Atheists made up a mere 10% of the population, but in the East they made up 70%.

There is still the problem of Skinheads in Germany. About 7 murders a year are attributed to Skinheads and their violent movement. The number of Skinhead related murders in the USA are triple that number. American seems to have a larger problem with White Supremacy than Germany currently! However, Israel has an even higher number of murders than even the US.

Skinhead are called as such because they shave their heads. They are often tattooed with swastikas. They certainly have many swastikas in decorations around them and give the Hitler salute. There are maybe 10,000 members in the new Nazi party. They are very right wing and believe foreigners should not be allowed to have any sort of benefits.

Overall though, things are looking good for Germany. They are part of the European Union or the EU. The EU does about 40% of their trade with Germany these days. Germans have taken increasing responsibility for their part in History. The Holocaust is taught in Germany, although Dominic isn't sure of the exact curriculum. Germany is also leading the way in the Environmental Movement in Europe.

Final Exam

1) **Model Based. Why Germany was Divided and Reunited**
2) **What the Nazi's Place in German History was. Was it part of the German Character or a Unique happening**

My argument was that it was a unique happening—although the German Character contributed to the perfect storm. Other factors: Nationalism, Pushing of Boundaries, Industrial Revolution, Civil War, Being Blamed for WWI, Unstable Government, Nazism, Propaganda and Hitler himself.

Joachim Fest's Book *Plotting Hitler's Death*
Metropolitan Books, NY 1996

Joachim Fest's book *Plotting Hitler's Death* is an ambitious book that attempts to describe the German Resistance to Hitler. This book expresses how the men who led the German Resistance to Hitler gained a moral victory even though the failed to actually assassinate Hitler. The book begins with the most famous attempt on Hitler's life, July 20, 1944 and then retraces what led up to it, beginning with the time Hitler was gaining power. The book does not have much about the resistance to Hitler prior to him being elected Chancellor because there wasn't much protest or press surrounding him until much later. He was jailed before his time as Chancellor, but even that was not enough to stop him from carrying out his grand plans. It wasn't until after WWII that the protests against Hitler and the assignation attempts would be officially called a Resistance.

The basic theme of the book was that the attempt was "a plot that failed but achieved moral victory." In other words, these men can be commended for their admirable efforts even if it changed very little in the grand scheme of things. Fest felt that even if they had succeeded in killing Hitler, that it would have done very little good once the Nazi's were in power. Fest even went as far as to say that these men felt a deep moral and spiritual need to get rid of Hitler even when it appeared to be too late.

Fest jumps from different people and events as he answers questions such as who were the conspirators and why did they resist

Hitler? The people who resisted Hitler came from a number of places, but there was only one group that had enough organization or power to pose much of a threat—the career military men. The resistance did, however, include lawyers, students, union leaders, field marshals, politicians, journalists and even bookbinders. There were men such as Axel von dem Bussche, who was enthusiastic for Hitler until he saw the mass murder of the Jews in October of 1942. Then he, like others, was eager to join the resistance once they saw what was really happening.

The essence of the resistance before the war was minimal. There were a few early conspirators who did try to become allies with England, but due to a lack of communication nothing was really ever accomplished. The conspirators were discouraged by their lack of support and ended up sitting back and waiting for the right time to act.

On December 26, 1943, Col. Claus Schenk von Stauffenberg made his first attempt on Hitler's life at the Wolf's Lair, which was Hitler's headquarters near Rastenberg in East Prussia. The meeting was, unfortunately, canceled and the next meeting saw Stauffenberg unable to complete his mission. Finally, on July 20, 1944 Colonel Stauffenberg went to a meeting with Hitler and the other Army Generals. There, he successfully planted a bomb that was meant to kill Hitler and the other leaders as well. The bomb did go off after Stauffenberg left the building, but no one, including Hitler, was killed.

It was Fest's conclusion that these conspirators lacked any real organization and relied too much on their chain of command. It was their inability to act swiftly and precisely that led them to fail. Some of conspirators committed suicide once they heard that Hitler was alive, not wishing to face his wrath.   In he was indeed angry. More than 7,000 people were arrested after the failed attempt. Most were involved in the plot, but some were not. Nearly 5,000 people were executed over the years that followed. Some of the men that were implicated were Stauffenberg, Rommel, Schlabrendorff and Hellendorf.

The overall style of the book was very confusing. Fest wrote it in chronological order, but the chapters are divided into the various groups and movements. While Fest focused on the plot to kill Hitler, there was a lot of excess material on Hitler's Rise to power that didn't really need to be there. Fest claimed in The New York Times

Review of Books that is him aim was, "not so much to convey new information as to recount an old story in the light of the latest research." The book was indeed well researched. There was a great many names and overwhelming amount of facts. Unfortunately, there were some things that Fest assumed that the reader would already know and so it made the overall picture a bit fuzzy. Reading the summery in Spielbvogel's book helped put it all into perspective. The information was basically the same, but much shorter and clearer.

Joachim Fest compiled a lot of interesting information in this book, but just like the conspirators, he lacked clever organization. Fest did accomplish his goal in shedding new light on an old story, so it was worth reading.